SALSA
AND
RELATED GENRES

SALSA
AND
RELATED GENRES

A Bibliographical Guide

Compiled by
Rafael Figueroa

Music Reference Collection, Number 38

Greenwood Press
Westport, Connecticut • London

Library of Congress Cataloging-in-Publication Data

Figueroa, Rafael.
   Salsa and related genres : a bibliographical guide / compiled by
Rafael Figueroa.
     p. cm.—(Music reference collection, ISSN 0736-7740 ; no.
38)
   Includes bibliographical references and indexes.
   ISBN 0-313-27883-0 (alk. paper)
   1. Salsa—Bibliography. I. Title. II. Series.
ML128.S24F5   1992
016.78162'969729—dc20   92-23778

British Library Cataloguing in Publication Data is available.

Library of Congress Catalog Card Number: 92-23778
ISBN: 0-313-27883-0
ISSN: 0736-7740

First published in 1992

Greenwood Press, 88 Post Road West, Westport, CT 06881
An imprint of Greenwood Publishing Group, Inc.

The paper used in this book complies with the
Permanent Paper Standard issued by the National
Information Standards Organization (Z39.48-1984).

10 9 8 7 6 5 4 3 2 1

What is now presented. . . as something new, capable of producing new thrills, is not something which has been improvised as a tourist attraction, but a spiritual achievement of a people that has struggled during four centuries to find a medium of expression.

Emilio Grenet (1930)

Contents

Introduction

Salsa is the tip of an iceberg. Often it is the first musical impression the non-Latin world receives of Latin American culture. Salsa has a growing number of listeners all over the world; professional and amateur musicians are performing it regularly for non-hispanic audiences; colleges and universities have salsa or salsa-related topics in their curriculum; salsa festivals and jazz festivals including salsa are a regular feature in most European cities. Without a doubt salsa is experiencing a boom. This is not, however, an overnight success. Latin music has long been the single most important influence on popular music in the United States.[1] Following in this tradition, salsa and its related universe of styles are becoming an important force on the contemporary music scene, proceeding along the same path as did other popular genres: from ethnic origins to urban underground to world-wide acceptance and, then, to academic study.

This path of course, is not free of obstacles. Universities concentrate mainly on classical or folk music with not much in between,[2] and it is still difficult for some people to think that popular music is worthy of academic study. Fortunately, this view is changing. This volume tries to fill a gap in the study of one of the most important

---

[1] For more on this, see Roberts, John Storm, **The Latin Tinge** (item 41).

[2] For a good introduction to the problems of popular music research, see Blum, Joseph, **Problems of Salsa Research** (item 127).

types of Latin American music and now of the music of the world. Of course, academicians may use more technically correct names, such as "Afro-Hispanic Music of the Antilles," but the word **salsa** (Spanish for sauce, typically a hot condiment) has really caught on, just as jazz and rock did years ago, in spite of its inaccuracy. This book is not the forum to debate the use of the name. Suffice is to say that the title salsa was chosen for this work because it is the term that best represents this music for the non-Latin world. Salsa represents a body of sound that emerged from the Antilles (Cuba, Puerto Rico, and Dominican Republic) as a result of the meeting of European and African cultures, just as jazz did, but on a different basis. This music is related, of course, to other musical genres of Latin America and the Caribbean, but it stands on its own with strong roots in its tradition - a musical tradition based on a unique rhythmic unit (the **clave**) that blends in itself the European and African heritage and provides the ground to build a highly complex poly-rhythmic and contrapuntal structure of all the instruments.

The purpose of this book is to present materials about this musical genre that are available for the non-Latin world. To this end, special emphasis was made on English-language sources. Materials in Spanish were included only when an English equivalent was not available and, even then, preference was given to materials produced in the United States or Puerto Rico. All magazines cited are published in the United States unless otherwise indicated.

The compilation was made as universal as possible, as the interests of a musician are not the same as those of a musicologist, an anthropologist, a journalist or necessarily those of the devoted listener. Books, articles, dissertations, specific entries in encyclopedias, videos and liner notes are included.

People familiar with the field will note many important gaps. This is due to the lack of availability of sources, which continues to be a major problem when dealing with this area of knowledge. Many sources included here are difficult to find because they do not fall into the usual fields of bibliographical data. Hispanic publications, self-published books, and materials for musicians are not normally indexed or classified in libraries or information services. They tend to go unnoticed in spite of their value and often are found only by chance. That is why the work of programs like CONCLAVE are very important, in providing the basis for an efficient flow of information about this neglected field. CONCLAVE[3] opened its databases to this researcher and made available most of the materials to review for this book.

Some considerations about the structure and use of this book follow:

1. The book is arranged in four parts. The first part deals with works reflecting a general point of view, covering whole areas or countries. The focus of the second part is on specific styles, genres and rhythms. The third section covers biographical information, and the last addresses topics related to playing, teaching, or arranging for the various instruments. Each section begins with a listing of general works and is then followed by the intrinsic topics arranged in alphabetical order. (For the most part, divisions of the first section are national; those of the second are styles and genres; the third, names of musicians; the fourth, instruments.) Each entry includes bibliographical citations alphabetized by author (by title for anonymous sources). In the biographical section record reviews follow other sources, listed alphabetically by journal under each record title. (The record company where known, is indicated parenthetically following the title.)

2. Entries are numbered sequentially regardless of section and topical divisions. The numbers used for cross-referencing and in the index refer to these entry numbers and not to pages. For the most part, abbreviations are consciously avoided for the sake of clarity.

3. Normally, Spanish names have three parts - personal name, father's last name, and mother's last name - and are alphabetized under the second name, not the last as in English. However, in special cases, a popular Hispanic musician may be better known by the last part of his name. For example, Dámaso Pérez Prado would correctly be listed under Pérez, not Prado, as he usually is named in non-Latin media.

---

[3]   CONCLAVE in Spanish means "with clave," but also, both in English and Spanish, has the meaning of a meeting or gathering.

Taking into consideration that this might be confusing for English-speaking readers, we alphabetized all these names the correct Spanish way but entered a cross-reference at the place where a non-Latin reader might try to find it.

4. Accents and other diacritical marks are presented here as they would normally appear in a Spanish context. They do not change alphabetizing or meaning and are included to familiarize non-Latin readers with the correct spelling and to avoid confusion.

5. Most of the entries have self-explanatory titles or they are general profiles. Otherwise, brief annotations are provided.

I should like to give special thanks to Greenwood Press for making this book possible and to the CONCLAVE program, whose work is fundamental in this moment of the blossoming of the Afro-Hispanic Music of the Antilles on the contemporary scene. Also special thanks go to Jorge Carmona and Bernardo Palombo for providing the support and inspiring the confidence to enable me to accomplish this project.

More than anything, this is a work of love for the music that has filled my life with joy and happiness. I hope that it will prove itself useful and also increase the thirst for more knowledge and academic effort in this field. Suggestions of additional references that should be included in a future edition of this book, would be appreciated. These should be forwarded to Rafael Figueroa/CONCLAVE, 245 Eighth Ave. # 191, New York, NY 10011.

¡Hasta pronto!

SALSA
AND
RELATED GENRES

1

General

1. Dratch, Howard and Eugene Rosow (Directors). **Routes of Rhythm with Harry Belafonte**. Los Angeles, CA: Cultural Research and Communication, 1990 (Video, color, 3 programs of 58 minutes each, Dist. by Cinema Guild, NY).

> Excellent from the documentary point of view. Appearances of Rubén Blades, Celia Cruz, los Van Van, Irakere and others make it even more valuable, even though it is sometimes more concerned with the sociological and historical aspects than with the music itself.

2. Durán, Gustavo. **Recordings of Latin American Songs and Dances: An Annotated Selective List of Popular and Folk-Popular Music**. Washington, D.C.: Pan American Union, 1950 (2nd. Edition, revised and enlarged by Gilbert Chase) 92 pp.

> Useful not because of the dated information on recordings but for the concise entries on rhythms and styles. Sections on Cuba (p. 38-48), the Dominican Republic (p. 48-50) and Puerto Rico (p. 75-78).

General (cont.)

> 3. Manuel, Peter. **Popular Musics of the Non-Western World: An Introductory Survey**. New York, NY: Oxford University Press, 1988. 287 pp.
>
> > Chapter 2 "Latin America and the Caribbean" provides a succinct and well-documented introduction to the salsa musical area with a well-thought approach to the concept of popular music.
>
> 4. Roberts, John Storm. **Black Music of Two Worlds.** New York: Morrow Paperbacks, 1974. 282 pp.
>
> > General and pioneer work dealing with African-derived music as a whole.

Cuba

> 5. Carpentier, Alejo. **La Música en Cuba.** México: Fondo de Cultura Económica, 1946 (Col. Tierra Firme, 19) 282 pp.
>
> > Emphasis on music of the European tradition with spare information on popular styles. Based on primary sources.
>
> 6. Casanova Oliva, Ana Victoria. **Problemática Organológica Cubana: Crítica a la Sistemática de los Instrumentos Musicales.** Havana: Casa de las Américas, 1988. 209 pp.
>
> > Thorough classification of Cuban instruments.
>
> 7. Díaz Ayala, Cristóbal. **Música Cubana: Del Areyto a la Nueva Trova**. San Juan, Puerto Rico: Editorial Cubanacán, 1981. 383 pp.
>
> > Comprehensive historical information on the music scene in Cuba from 1492 to 1980. A lot of information, sometimes too anecdotal. Very useful however.

8. Elí Rodríguez, Victoria. "Apuntes sobre la Creación Musical Actual en Cuba". **Revista de Música Latino Americana/Latin American Music Review.** Vol. 10, no. 2 (Fall/Winter 1989) p. 287-297.

It covers the whole spectrum of Cuban music with a section on dance music that includes an inventory of the latest innovations in popular Cuban music.

9. Galán, Natalio. **Cuba y sus Sones.** Valencia, Spain: PreTextos, 1983. 359 pp.

Beginning in 1650, this is a history of Afro-Cuban genres (not only **son** like the title says). The author is sometimes too worried about the legends behind the music.

10. León, Argeliers. **Del Canto y el Tiempo.** Havana: Editorial Letras Cubanas, 1984. 329 pp.

Essential work by one of the most important research-ers on Afro-Cuban Music. It covers a wide spectrum from the folkloric roots based on African music to more contemporary aspects like mambo or cha-cha-chá. Facsimiles of original sheet music, lyrics and transcriptions add to its value.

11. Manuel, Peter. "Marxism, Nationalism and Popular Music in Revolutionary Cuba". **Popular Music** (Liverpool, England) Vol. 6, no. 2 (May 1987) p. 161-178.

Analysis of the relationship "between the reality of popular music in Cuba and the theories and attitudes toward it expressed by officials, bureaucrats, musi-cians, musicologists, journalists and consumers."

Cuba (cont.)

12. Orovio, Helio. **Diccionario de la Música Cubana: Biográfico y Técnico.** Havana: Editorial Letras Cubanas, 1981. 442 pp.

> Succinct and all-encompassing reference work of Cuban music, providing with general but useful information on a myriad of terms, instruments, genres, composers and performers. Invaluable.

13. Ortiz Fernández, Fernando. **La Africanía de la Música Folklórica de Cuba.** Havana: Ed. Universitaria, 1965. 477 pp.

> Detailed discussion of the African elements in Cuban folk music. Invaluable transcriptions of batá rhythms and santería melodies. Thorough and well-documented as usual coming from don Fernando. Essential.

14. Ortiz, Fernando. **Los Bailes y el Teatro de los Negros en el Folklore de Cuba**. Havana: Editorial Letras Cubanas, 1981. 603 pp.

> Ethnographic description of the different elements of the Afro-Cuban religions with special emphasis on dance and music.

15. Sagramoso, Uberto (Director). **Hecho en Cuba**. New York: Interamerican Productions, 1988 (Video, color, dist. by Videoteca del Sur, NY).

> Informal documentary on popular Cuban music. It offers some first hand data on the post-revolutionary scene: Los Van Van, Arturo Sandoval, Tumba Francesa and others.

16. Santos, John. Liner notes to **Music of Cuba.** Produced by Verna Gillis. New York: Folkways, 1985.

17. Sulsbrück, Birger. "Latin Percussion: Cuban Musical Styles". **Jazz Educators Journal** (December 1987/January 1988) p. 41-44.

18. Sulsbrück, Birger. "Latin Percussion: Cuban Musical Styles. Part II". **Jazz Educators Journal** (February/March 1988) p. 34-36

Dominican Republic

19. Alberti, Luis. **De Música y Orquestas Bailables Dominicanas 1910-1959**. Santo Domingo: Editora Taller, 1975. 159 pp.

> Personal recollection of the popular music scene in the Dominican Republic (1910-1959) by one of its most important composers and band leaders. Plenty of musical data about merengue with piano scores of some of Alberti's compositions.

20. Andrade, Manuel José. **Folklore de la República Dominicana**. Ciudad Trujillo: Universidad de Santo Domingo, 1948. 2 vols. (ITS Publicaciones, 54)

21. Coopersmith, Jacob Maurice. **Music and Musicians of the Dominican Republic. Música y Músicos de la República Dominicana**. Washington, D.C.: Division of Music and Visual Arts, Dept. of Cultural Affairs, Pan American Union, 1949. 146 pp. (Music Series, 15)

> Overview of Dominican music, covering song and dance forms, instruments, composers, etc.

22. Davis, Martha Ellen. "Aspectos de la Influencia Africana en la Música Tradicional Dominicana". **Boletín del Museo del Hombre Dominicano** (Santo Domingo, Dominican Republic) No. 13, p. 255-292

23. Gillis, Verna. Liner notes to **The Island of Española. Music from the Dominican Republic**. Produced by Verna Gillis. New York, NY: Folkways Records, 1976

Dominican Republic (cont.)

24. Gillis, Verna. Liner notes to **The Island of Quisqueya: Music from the Dominican Republic**. Produced by Verna Gillis. New York, NY: Folkways Records, 1976

25. González Canahuate, Almanzor. **Recopilación de la Música Popular Dominicana**. Santo Domingo: 1989. 456 pp.

26. Hernández, Julio Alberto. **Música Folklórica y Popular de la República Dominicana**. Santo Domingo, 1964

27. Hernández, Julio Alberto. **Música Tradicional Dominicana**. Santo Domingo: Julio D. Postigo, 1969. 202 pp. (Colección Artistas Dominicanos, 1)

> Panoramic view of folk and popular styles. 100 pages of scores.

28. Lizardo Barinas, Fradique. **La Canción Folklórica en Santo Domingo**. San Cristóbal: Imprenta Benemérita, 1958. 83 pp. (Publ. de la Sociedad Folklórica Dominicana, 1)

29. Marks, Morton and Isidro Bobadilla. Liner notes to **Afro-Dominican Music from San Cristóbal, Dominican Republic**. New York, NY: Folkways Records, 1983

Puerto Rico

30. Alvarez Nazario, Manuel. **El Elemento Afronegroide en el Español de Puerto Rico**. San Juan: Instituto de Cultura Puertorriqueña, 1974 (2a.ed.) 491 pp.

> Even tough this is a book dealing primarily with language, the chapter titled "Música y bailes" (p. 284-318) provides a lot of information on instruments, dances and songs.

31. Bloch, Peter. **La-le-lo-lai: Puerto Rican Music and Its Performers**. New York: Plus Ultra Educational Publishers, 1973. 197 pp.

> Superficial introduction to Puerto Rican music with an emphasis on the whiter mountain music. Full of anecdotes.

32. Dufrasne-González, J. Emanuel. **La Homogeneidad de la Música Caribeña: Sobre la Música Comercial y Popular de Puerto Rico**. Ph. D. diss., University of California, Los Angeles, 1985. 478 pp.

> Ethnomusicological research emphasizing the similarities of different salsa-related genres. It covers organology, performance practices, terminology, and even, popularity. Good first-hand information mixed with already published data. Extensive coverage of chordophones covering construction, tunings, and stringings (Puerto Rican cuatro and Cuban tres among others). Also information on organology and construction of bomba drums. Musical transcriptions of plenas, bomba songs and drumming patterns.

33. López Cruz, Francisco. **La Música Folklórica de Puerto Rico**. Sharon, CT: Troutman Press, 1967. 203 pp.

> Limited ethnomusicological approach. Chapters "Los Bailes de Bomba" (p. 47-62); "La Plena" (p. 65-96); "La Guaracha" (p. 99-119) offer musical examples of songs and rhythmic accompaniments. Good coverage of the cuatro.

34. Malavet Vega, Pedro. **La Vellonera está Directa: Felipe Rodríguez (La Voz) y los Años '50**. Dominican Republic: Author, 1985 (2ª ed.) 487 pp.

Puerto Rico (cont.)

> Even though this is a book about a non-salsa singer, Felipe Rodríguez, the author's kaleidoscopical style allows a lot of important musical data relevant to the salsa tradition to appear in this recollection of Puerto Rican popular music of the '50s.

35. Muñoz Santaella, María Luisa. **La Música en Puerto Rico: Panorama Histórico-Cultural.** Sharon, CT: The Troutman Press, 1966 (Puerto Rico: Realidad y Anhelo, 3) 167 pp.

> Brief description of the folk elements of hispanic and african origin in Puerto Rican music plus some short biographies of nineteenth Century danza composers. Otherwise Muñoz' approach is biased towards the music of European tradition. It includes a very limited and dated bibliography. It was originally an Ed. D. dissertation for the Teachers College, Columbia University, 1958.

U.S.A.

36. Agudelo, Carlos. "Still Dirty Dancing after All these Years". **The Village Voice** (August 9, 1988) p. 24

37. Brown, David Hilary. **Garden in the Machine: Afro-Cuban Sacred Art and Performance in Urban New Jersey and New York**. Ph. D. diss., Yale University, 1989. 627 pp. (2 vols.)

> Provides descriptions of contemporary performance practices of Santería in the New York area.

38. Cornelius, Steven Harry. **The Convergence of Power: An Investigation into the Music Liturgy of Santería in New York City.** Ph. D. diss., University of California, Los Angeles, 1989. 358 pp.

This book deals with the communication process of music in Santería, through a taxonomic study of musical instruments, formal analysis of musical structure and the analysis of the musician's role within the ritual.

39. Cortés, Féliz, Angel Falcón and Juan Flores. "The Cultural Expression of Puerto Ricans in New York: A Theoretical Perspective and Critical Review". **Latin American Perspectives**. Vol. 3, no. 3 (Summer 1976) p. 117-152

40. Reyes-Schramm, Adelaida. **The Role of Music in the Interaction of Black Americans and Hispanics in New York City's East Harlem.** Ph. D. diss., Columbia University, 1975. 273 pp.

41. Roberts, John Storm. **The Latin Tinge: The Impact of Latin American Music on the United States.** New York: Original Music, 1985. 246 pp. (Reprint of 1979 edition)

A classic even though it has some deficiencies. A remarkable source of information.

42. Roseman, Marina. "The New Rican Village: Artists in Control of the Image-Making Machinery". **Revista de Música Latino Americana/Latin American Music Review.** Vol. 4, no. 1 (Spring/Summer 1983) p. 132

43. Singer, Roberta. **My Music is Who I am and What I Do: Latin Popular Music and Identity in New York City.** Ph. D. diss., Indiana University, 1982. 265 pp.

A study of music as a way to express and reinforce identity among Latins in New York City.

44. Singer, Roberta and Robert Friedman. "Puerto Rican and Cuban Musical Expression in New York". Liner notes to **Caliente=Hot.** New York: New World Records / Recorded Anthology of American Records, 1977

U.S.A. (cont.)

45. Singer, Roberta. "Tradition and Innovation in Contemporary Latin Popular Music in New York City". **Revista de Música Latino Americana/Latin American Music Review.** Vol. 4, no. 2 (Fall/Winter 1983) p. 183-202

46. Struman, Janer L. "Advertising and Latin Music at a New York City Jazz Club: Interrelationships that Shape the Musical Event". **Current Musicology.** No. 37/38 (1984) p. 159-166

> Socioeconomic analysis of the long standing series *Salsa meets Jazz* at the Village Gate in New York City. Well documented.

47. Wolfe, Tom. "The Hidden World of Up-Tempo Latin!". **The New York Herald Tribune** (June 20, 1965) p. 6-9

2

Styles and Rhythms

Afro-Cuban (Santería)

48. "Afro-Cuban Music". **The Penguin Encyclopedia of Popular Music.** Donald Clarke (ed.) London: Viking, 1989. p. 11

49. Loza, Steven. **Music and the Afro-Cuban Experience: A Survey of the Yoruba Tradition in Cuba in Relation to the Origin, Form, and Development of Contemporary Afro-Cuban Rhythms.** Master's Thesis: University of California, Los Angeles, 1979

See **Batá Drums**

Bachata

50. Pacini-Hernández, Deborah. "*Cantando la Cama Vacía:* Love, Sexuality and Gender Relationship in Dominican *Bachata*". **Popular Music** (Liverpool, England) Vol. 9, no. 3 (October 1990) p. 351-367

51. Pacini-Hernández, Deborah. **Music of Marginality: Social Identity and Class in Dominican Bachata.** Ph. D. diss. Cornell University, 1989

Bachata (cont.)

52. Pacini-Hernández, Deborah. "Social Identity and Class in Bachata, an Emerging Dominican Popular Music". **Revista de Música Latino Americana/Latin American Music Review.** Vol. 10, no. 1 (Spring/Summer 1989) p. 69-91

Bolero

53. "Bolero". **The Penguin Encyclopedia of Popular Music.** Donald Clarke (ed.) London: Viking, 1989. p. 132

54. Díaz Ayala, Cristóbal. "Descripción y Narración en el Bolero Puertorriqueño". **Revista Musical Puertorriqueña.** No. 3 (January/June 1988) p. 32-51

Analyzes lyrics of Puerto Rican boleros.

55. Silverman, Chuck. "Latin Beat". **Rhythm** (May 1989) p. 50-51

Bolero applications for drum-set.

Bomba

56. "Bomba". **The Penguin Encyclopedia of Popular Music.** Donald Clarke (ed.) London: Viking, 1989. p. 132-133

57. McCoy, James A. **The Bomba and Aguinaldo of Puerto Rico as They Have Evolved from Indigenous, African and European Cultures.** Ph. D. diss., Florida State University, 1968. 185 pp.

58. Vega Drouet, Héctor. **Historical and Ethnological Survey on Probable African Origins of the Puerto Rican Bomba, Including a Description of Santiago Apóstol Festivities at Loíza Aldea.** Ph. D. diss., Wesleyan University, 1979. 170 pp.

59. Vega Drouet, Héctor. "The Bomba and Plena: Africa Retained in Music and Dance of Puerto Rico". **Caribe New York.** Vol. 7, no. 1/2 (1983) p. 42-43

60. Vega Drouet, Héctor. **Some Musical Forms of African Descendants in Puerto Rico: Bomba, Plena and Rosario Francés**. Master's Thesis, Hunter College, 1969

> Scholarly musical analysis of bomba and plena plus descriptions of choreography and performance practices.

Boogaloo

61. "Boogaloo". **The Penguin Encyclopedia of Popular Music.** Donald Clarke (ed.) London: Viking, 1989. p. 136

Cha-cha-chá

62. Armstrong, Derick. "The Charanga and the Cha Cha Cha". **Jazz Monthly.** Vol. 5, no. 3 (May 1959) p. 6-7, 31; Vol. 5, no. 4 (June 1959) p. 7-9

63. "Cha Cha Chá". **The Penguin Encyclopedia of Popular Music.** Donald Clarke (ed.) London: Viking, 1989. p. 219-220

64. Norton, Pauline. "Cha Cha Chá". **The New Grove Dictionary of American Music.** H. Wiley Hitchcock and Stanley Sadie (eds.) London: Macmillan Press, 1986. Vol. 1, p. 383

65. Silverman, Chuck. "Latin Beat". **Rhythm** (April 1989) p. 56

> Cha-cha-chá applications for the drum-set.

66. Terry, Walter. "The Conga, the Pachanga, and the Cha Cha Cha". **Saturday Review** (September 4, 1968) p. 59

Charanga

67. "Charanga". **The Penguin Encyclopedia of Popular Music.** Donald Clarke (ed.) London: Viking, 1989. p. 223-224

See   62. Armstrong, Derick. "The Charanga and the Cha Cha Cha"

Comparsa

68. Schloss, Andrew. Liner notes to **Carnival in Cuba.** New York: Ethnic Folkways, 1981

Conga (Rhythm)

69. "Conga". **The New Grove Dictionary of Jazz.** Barry Kernfeld (ed.) London: Macmillan Press, 1988. Vol. 1, p. 242

70. Kernfeld, Barry and Pauline Norton. "Conga". **The New Grove Dictionary of American Music.** H. Wiley Hitchcock and Stanley Sadie (eds.) London: Macmillan Press, 1986. Vol. 1. p. 486

71. Martínez Acosta, Pedro. "Congas en la Provincia Cubana de Camagüey". **Ensayos de Música Latinoamericana: Selección del Boletín de Música de la Casa de las Américas.** Havana: Casa de las Américas, 1982. p. 287-292

See   66. Terry, Walter. "The Conga, the Pachanga and the Cha Cha Cha"

Conjunto

72. "Conjunto". **The Penguin Encyclopedia of Popular Music.** Donald Clarke (ed.) London: Viking, 1989. p. 274

Danzón

73. Fernández Valdés, Olga. "En Memoria del Danzón". **A Pura Guitarra y Tambor.** Santiago de Cuba: Editorial Oriente 1984. p. 38-39

Historical recollection of the origins of Danzón.

74. Santos, John. Liner notes to **The Cuban** *Danzón***: Its Ancestors and Descendants.** New York: Folkways, 1982 (Produced by Andrew Schloss)

75. Urfé, Odilio. **El Danzón.** Cuba: Consejo Nacional de Cultura, 1965

76. Urfé, Odilio. **Síntesis Histórica del Danzón.** Havana: Biblioteca Nacional Jose Martí, < n.d. >

See   296. Castillo Faílde, Osvaldo. **Miguel Faílde, Creador Musical del Danzón.**

Latin Jazz

77. "Afro-Cuban Jazz". **The New Grove Dictionary of Jazz.** Barry Kernfeld (ed.) London: Macmillan Press, 1988. Vol. 1, p. 7-8

78. Agudelo, Carlos. "Un 'Swing' Tropical". **Más.** Vol. 2, no. 3 (January/February 1991) p. 55

79. "Cubop". **The Penguin Encyclopedia of Popular Music.** Donald Clarke (ed.) London: Viking, 1989. p. 306

80. Kernfeld, Barry. "Latin Jazz". **The New Grove Dictionary of American Music.** H. Wiley Hitchcock and Stanley Sadie (eds.) London: Macmillan Press, 1986. Vol. 3, p. 16

81. "Latin Jazz". **The New Grove Dictionary of Jazz.** Barry Kernfeld (ed.) London: Macmillan Press, 1988. Vol. 2, p. 13

Latin Jazz (cont.)

82. Leymarie, Isabelle. "Salsa and Latin Jazz". **Hot Sauces: Latin & Caribbean Pop.** Billy Bergman and others. New York: Quarto, 1985 p. 95-115

83. O'Farrill, Chico. "Latin Drumming in Jazz". **Jazz.** Vol. 5, no. 12 (1966) p. 19

84. **Paquito D'Rivera Music Minus Me.** Weehawken, NJ: The Havana-New York Music Co. (Booklet and tape set)

> Music-minus-one treatment of some of Paquito's hits. Good for all melodic instruments.

85. Pinckney, Warren R., Jr. "Puerto Rican Jazz and the Incorporation of Folk Music: An Analysis of New Musical Directions". **Revista de Música Latino Americana/Latin American Music Review.** Vol. 10, no. 2 (Fall/Winter 1989) p. 236-266

> Covers jazz in Puerto Rico and how it naturally blends into a *sui generis* form of Latin jazz.

86. Schuller, Gunther. "Afro-Cuban Jazz". **The New Grove Dictionary of American Music.** H. Wiley Hitchcock and Stanley Sadie (eds.) London: Macmillan Press, 1986. Vol. 1, p. 21

87. Smith, Arnold Jay. "Salute to Jazz Latino". **Down Beat** (September 7, 1978) p. 59

Latin Rock

88. Cobham, Billy. "Drum Machine Techniques: Latin Rock Rhythms". **Keyboard Magazine** (April 1985) p. 74

89. Latham, R. "Latin Rock Patterns". **Modern Drummer.** Vol. 6 (May 1982) p. 94-95

90. Sciarrino, Johnny and Walfredo de los Reyes. **Salsa Rock: A Complete Guide for Blending the Drum-set with the Latin Rhythm Section.** Sherman Oaks, CA: Alfred Publishing, 1978. 24 pp.

> Covers salsa-disco, ñañigo, comparsa and patterns in 3/4, 5/4 and 7/4.

Mambo

91. Goldberg, Norbert. "South of the Border: The Mambo". **Modern Drummer** (August/September 1979) p. 36-37

92. "Mambo". **The Penguin Encyclopedia of Popular Music.** Donald Clarke (ed.) London: Viking, 1989. p. 758

93. Norton, Pauline. "Mambo". **The New Grove Dictionary of American Music.** H. Wiley Hitchcock and Stanley Sadie (eds.) London: Macmillan Press, 1986. Vol. 3, p. 165

94. Rae, John. "South of the Border: Mambo on the Drum Set". **Modern Drummer.** Vol. 5 (December 1981/January 1982) p. 52-53

95. Salazar, Max. "Who Invented the Mambo? Part I and II". **Mambo Express Magazine.** Vol. 3, no. 20 (June 1990) p. 4-8; Vol. 3, no. 21 (July 1990) p. 4-6

> Interesting summary of the discussion of the origins of mambo.

96. Silverman, Chuck. "Latin Beat: More Mambo/Bongo Bell Patterns". **Rhythm** (April 1990) p. 46-47

Merengue

97. Austerlitz, Paul. **A History of the Dominican Merengue, Highlighting the Role of the Saxophone.** Master's Thesis, Wesleyan University, 1986

Merengue (cont.)

> 98. Castillo, José del and Manuel A. García Arévalo. **Antología del Merengue.** Santo Domingo: Banco Antillano, 1989. 91 pp.
>
> > Excellent overview of the genre from the turn of the century to the present. Bilingual text.
>
> 99. Cocks, Jay. "You Can't Stop Dancing: A New Merengue Craze Heats Up the Club Game". **Time** (October 6, 1986) No. 128. p. 91
>
> 100. Kernfeld, Barry. "Merengue". **The New Grove Dictionary of American Music.** H. Wiley Hitchcock and Stanley Sadie (eds.) London: Macmillan Press, 1986. Vol. 3, p. 214
>
> 101. McLane, Daisann. "Dance Till You Drop Merengue". **The New York Times.** Vol. 140 (January 6, 1981) sec. 2 p.H28
>
> 102. Medrano, Hugo. "*Merengue's* New Moves". **Américas** (September/October 1986) p. 54-55
>
> 103. "Merengue". **The Penguin Encyclopedia of Popular Music.** Donald Clarke (ed.) London: Viking, 1989. p. 793-794
>
> 104. Santos, John. "South of the Border: the Merengue". **Modern Drummer.** Vol. 12, no. 1 (January 1988) p. 108-109

Mozambique

> 105. Santos, John. "South of the Border: the Mozambique". **Modern Drummer.** Vol. 12, no. 3 (March 1988) p. 86-87
>
> 106. Silverman, Chuck. "Latin Beat: Mozambique - Part Two". **Rhythm** (November 1988) p. 54-55

107. Silverman, Chuck. "Latin Beat: Mozambique and Songo". **Rhythm** (October 1988) p. 48-49

108. Silverman, Chuck. "Latin Beat: Mozambique and Songo - Part III". **Rhythm** (December 1988) p. 54-55

109. Walden, M. Rupert. "Rock'n'Jazz Clinic: Gadd's Mozambique". **Modern Drummer** (March 1987) p. 42

Pachanga

110. Santos, John. "South of the Border: 'A Caballo'". **Modern Drummer** (March 1989) p. 72

> 'A Caballo' (on horseback) is the name given to the rhythm most associated with the pachanga.

111. Thompson, Robert Farris. "Portrait of the Pachanga, the Music, the Players, the Dancers". **Caribe.** Vol. 7, no. 1/2, p. 48

See   66. Terry, Walter. "The Conga, the Pachanga, and the Cha Cha Cha"

Plena

112. Blanco, Tomás. "Elogio de la Plena (Variaciones Boricuas)". **Revista del Ateneo.** (Puerto Rico) Vol. 3 (1935), p. 97-106

> Describes the music (rhythms and instruments) and the dance.

113. Echevarría Alvarado, Félix. **La Plena: Origen, Sentido y Desarrollo en el Folklore Puertorriqueño.** Santurce, Puerto Rico. 166 pp.

> Amateurish collection of anecdotes about plena, included here because it has some first-hand information about performers and composers unavailable elsewhere.

Plena (cont.)

> 114. Ferré, Rosario. "Una Conciencia Musical". **Cahiers du Monde Hispanique et Luso-Brésilien: Caravelle.** (Toulousse, France) No. 48 (1987) pp. 155-161
>
> > Personal recollection of the origins and history of plena by a native of Ponce the birthplace of this Puerto Rican rhythm. It includes the lyrics of one of the most famous plenas, "Mamita llegó el Obispo".

> 115. Flores, Juan. "Bumbún and the Beginnings of la Plena". **Centro de Estudios Puertorriqueños Bulletin.** Vol. 11, no. 3 (Spring 1988) p. 16-25

> 116. Rivera, Pedro and Susan Zeig (Directors). **Plena is Work, Plena is Song** (1989) 16mm/video, color, 37 minutes (Distributed by The Cinema Guild, NY)
>
> > Documentary that goes from the folk origins of plena up to its modern usage in Puerto Rico and N.Y.

> 117. Rodríguez Medina, Héctor. "The Puerto Rican Plena". **Highlights in Percussion.** Vol. 2, no. 2 (Summer 1988) p. 2

See   59. Vega Drouet, Héctor. "The Bomba and Plena: Africa Retained in Music and Dance of Puerto Rico."
60. Vega Drouet, Héctor. **Some Musical Forms of African Descendants in Puerto Rico: Bomba, Plena and Rosario Francés**

Pregón

> 118. Díaz Ayala, Cristóbal. **Si te Quieres por el Pico Divertir...: Historia del Pregón Musical Latinoamericano.** Puerto Rico: Editorial Cubanacán, 1988. 371 pp.

Rumba (Guaguancó)

119. Crook, Larry. "A Musical Analysis of the Cuban Rumba". **Revista de Música Latino Americana/Latin American Music Review.** Vol. 3, no. 1 (Spring/Summer 1982) p. 92-123

> Song texts, formal construction and percussion accompaniment are some of the topics.

120. Crook, Larry. **The Cuban Rumba.** Master's Thesis, University of Texas at Austin, 1980

121. Daniel, Yvonne Laverne Payne. **Ethnography of Rumba: Dance and Social Change in Contemporary Cuba.** Ph. D. diss., University of California, Berkeley, 1989. 461 pp.

> Studies rumba as a social force of identity in post-revolutionary Cuba, setting it within the social, economic, political, religious and aesthetic systems of contemporary Cuba. Emphasis is on the dance.

122. Gradante, William and Dean L. Root. "Rumba". **The New Grove Dictionary of American Music.** H. Wiley Hitchcock and Stanley Sadie (eds.) London: Macmillan Press, 1986. Vol. 4, p. 107

123. Manuel, Peter. "Formal Structure in Popular Music as a Reflection of Socio-Economic Change". **International Review of the Aesthetics and Sociology of Music.** Vol. 16, no. 2 (December 1985) p. 163-180

> Sociological analysis. One of the case studies is devoted to rumba.

124. "Rumba". **The Penguin Encyclopedia of Popular Music.** Donald Clarke (ed.) London: Viking, 1989. p. 1022

See   547. **Batá y Rumba**

Salsa

125. Arteaga Rodríguez, José. "Salsa y Violencia: Una Aproximación Sonoro-Histórica". **Revista Musical Puertorriqueña**. No. 4 (July December 1988) p. 20-33

Analysis of the lyrics looking for the relationship between music and violence.

126. Báez, Juan Carlos. **El Vínculo es la Salsa**. Caracas: Tropykos, 1989. 302 pp.

127. Blum, Joseph. "Problems of Salsa Research". **Ethnomusicology**. Vol. 22, no. 1 (January 1978) p. 137-149

Addresses the basic problems of musicologists studying salsa.

128. Duany, Jorge. "Popular Music in Puerto Rico: Toward an Anthropology of Salsa". **Revista de Música Latino Americana/Latin American Music Review**. Vol. 5, no. 2 (Fall/Winter 1984) p. 186-216

Sociological analysis of Salsa in Puerto Rico and New York City.

129. "Enter Salsa: Some Like it Hot". **Time**. 105 (May 5, 1975) p. 56-57

130. Fernández, Enrique. "Is Salsa Sinking?". **The Village Voice** (September 2, 1986) p. 18

131. Flores, Aurora. "Once-hot Biz of **Salsa** Sound is a Cold Note". **Daily News** (July 14, 1987) Business Section p. 1, 6

About the Fania label and its legal and economical problems. Excellent.

132. Francke, L.B. and Huck, J. "Hot New Sound of Salsa". **Newsweek**. 85 (May 26, 1975) p. 58-59

133. Gerard, Charley with Marty Sheller. **Salsa! The Rhythm of Latin Music.** Crown Point, IN: White Cliffs Media Co., 1989. 137 pp. (Includes a cassette of the musical examples)

> The most in-depth musical overview of Salsa as a genre. Highly recommended.

134. McKaie, Andy. "The History of Salsa/La Historia de la Salsa". **Fania All Stars Songbook.** Hialeah, FL: Columbia Pictures Publications, 1978. p. 16

135. Marre, Jeremy. **Salsa: Latin Music of New York and Puerto Rico.** Harcourt Films, 1979. Video, color (Part of the Series **Beats of the Heart**) (Distributed by Shanachie, Newton, NJ)

> Good documentary of salsa and its socio-political importance with interesting views from non-musicians Felipe Luciano and Jerry Massuci.

136. Pabón, Tony. "What Is Salsa?". **Latin New York** (October 1975) p. 33-34

137. Padilla, Félix M. "Salsa: Puerto Rican and Latino Music". **Journal of Popular Culture.** Vol. 24, no. 1 (Summer 1990) p. 87-104

138. Palmer, Robert. "Can Salsa Escape the Cultural Ghetto?". **The New York Times** (January 23, 1977) Sec. 2, p. 22-29

139. Pérez, Brittmarie Janson. "Political Facets of **Salsa**". **Popular Music** (Liverpool, England) Vol. 6, no. 2 (May 1987) p. 149-159

> Comparative analysis of political content in the lyrics of Rubén Blades and Pedro Altamiranda.

Salsa (cont.)

140. Roberts, John Storm. "Salsa". **The New Grove Dictionary of American Music.** H. Wiley Hitchcock and Stanley Sadie (eds.) London: Macmillan Press, 1986. Vol. 4, p. 125

141. Roberts, John Storm. "Salsa". **The New Grove Dictionary of Music and Musicians.** Stanley Sadie (ed.) London: Macmillan Press, 1980. Vol. 16, p. 430

142. Roberts, John Storm. "¡Salsa!: While We Weren't Looking, a Whole New Category of Music Has Somehow Managed to Sneak up on Us". **Stereo Review.** Vol. 34, no. 3 (March 1975) p. 64-68

143. Rondón, César Miguel. **El Libro de la Salsa: Crónica de la Música del Caribe Urbano.** Caracas, Venezuela: Editorial Arte, 1980. 345 pp.

> Without a doubt this is the most exhaustive work about the development of Salsa in New York since its origins after the decay of the Latin Big Bands of the 50's to its internationalization and success in the 70's. Important data about its development in the Continent specially Venezuela. Essential.

144. Salazar, Max. "Salsa Origins". **Latin Beat.** Vol. 1, no. 10 (November 1991) p. 9-11

145. "Salsa". **The Penguin Encyclopedia of Popular Music.** Donald Clarke (ed.) London: Viking, 1989. p. 1031-1032

146. Vargas, Barbara Kay. **Salsa Music: Primary Dimensions of Meaning in an Expressive Cultural Form -the Puerto Rican Experience as Chronicled Via Salsa Lyric Poetics.** Ph. D. diss., University of California, Irvine, 1989. 415 pp.

Tries to explain salsa meaning and the Puerto Rican experience in the Island and in the US through lyrics, exposing principal themes and topics. Transcribes the original lyrics in Spanish and translates them to English. Includes interviews.

See   82. Leymarie, Isabelle. "Salsa and Latin Jazz"
             586. Sulsbrück, Birger, Henrik Beck and Karsten Simonsen. **Salsa Session**

Santería

See   **Afro-Cuban**

Son

147. Cárdenas, Rocío. "Rafael Cueto: Una Historia del Son". **Revista Musical Puertorriqueña.** No. 2 (July/December 1987) p. 36-45

Good interview with a lot of data about son from one of the members of Trío Matamoros.

148. Feijóo, Samuel. **Son Cubano. Poesía General.** Havana: Letras Cubanas, 1986. 312 pp.

149. Linares, María Teresa. "El Sucu-sucu: Un Caso en el Área del Caribe". **Ensayos de Música Latinoamericana: Selección del Boletín de Música de la Casa de las Américas.** Clara Hernández (ed.) Havana: Casa de las Américas, 1982. p. 273-286

Ethnomusicological recollection of an almost extinct form of son montuno that still exists on Isla de Pinos in Cuba. Description of the dance, instruments, melodic and rhythmic structures with transcriptions of some of the melodies.

Son (cont.)

150. Orozco, Danilo. "El Son ¿Ritmo, Baile o Reflejo de la Personalidad Cultural Cubana?". **Musicología en Latinoamérica.** Zoila Gómez García (ed.) Havana: Ed. Arte y Literatura, 1984. p. 363-389

> Using a semiotic approach analyses the social and musical meaning of the **son.**

151. "Son". **The Penguin Encyclopedia of Popular Music.** Donald Clarke (ed.) London: Viking, 1989. p. 1094

152. Urfé, Odilio. "Bosquejo Histórico sobre el Origen y Desarrollo del Complejo Musical y Coreográfico del Son Cubano". **Ciclo del Son.** Alberto Muguercia (Compiler) Havana: Biblioteca Nacional José Martí (November 7, 1972)

Songo

153. Sanabria, Roberto 'Bobby'. "The Songo". **Modern Drummer** (April 1986) p. 76

154. Santos, John. "Latin Symposium: el Songo". **Modern Percussionist.** Vol. 2, no. 1 (1985-1986) p. 44-46

155. Santos, John. "South of the Border: More Songo for Drumset". **Modern Drummer** (December 1989) p. 98

156. Schaik, Tom van. "South of the Border: Variations on the Songo". **Modern Drummer** (April 1991) p. 90

157. Silverman, Chuck. "Latin Beat: Songo and the Accented Cáscara Pattern". **Rhythm.** Vol. 1, no. 9 (January 1989) p. 56-57

158. Silverman, Chuck. "Latin Beat". **Rhythm.** Vol. 1, no. 10 (February 1989) p. 64-65

See   107. Silverman, Chuck. "Latin Beat: Mozambique and Songo"
       108. Silverman, Chuck. "Latin Beat: Mozambique and Songo - Part III"

Tumba Francesa

159. Alén, Olavo R. **La Música de las Sociedades de Tumba Francesa en Cuba.** Havana, Cuba: Casa de las Américas, 1986/1987. 271 pp.

> Originally the author's Ph. D. dissertation, this book gives us a very thorough analysis of Tumba Francesa in Cuba, the ceremony, the rhythms, the instruments, the chants, etc. with musical transcriptions.

160. Fernández Valdés, Olga. "Fiesta de Tambores". **A Pura Guitarra y Tambor.** Santiago de Cuba: Editorial Oriente 1984. p. 46-49

> Succinct description and historical chronicle of Tumba Francesa. It provides some description on the instrumentation and the dance.

3

Biography

Acuña, Alex

161. "Acuña, Alex". **The New Grove Dictionary of Jazz.** Barry Kernfeld (ed.) London: Macmillan Press, 1988. Vol. 1, p. 4

162. Flans, Robyn. "Alex Acuña". **Modern Drummer.** Vol. 14, no. 10 (October 1990) p. 18-23, 80, 82, 84, 86, 88

163. McFall, Michael. "World Picture". **Rhythm** (April 1989) p. 36-44

> Interview with the West Coast gurus of the Latin percussion scene: Alex Acuña, Luis Conte and Efraín Toro.

Record Reviews
Alex Acuña & The Unknowns (JVC)
164. **Modern Drummer** (February 1991) p. 130

See   526. Acuña, Alex. **Drums and Percussion**

Alberto, José

165. Polacoloco. "Salsa Erótica". **Straight No Chaser.** No. 3 (Spring 1989) p. 25

166. Mieres, Jorge. "José Alberto se Define". **Canales.** Vol. 18, no. 343 (November 1990) p. 38-39

Armenteros, Alfredo "Chocolate"

167. "Armenteros, Alfredo 'Chocolate'". **The Penguin Encyclopedia of Popular Music.** Donald Clarke (ed.) London: Viking, 1989. p. 38

Arnaz, Desi

168. "Arnaz, Desi". **The Penguin Encyclopedia of Popular Music.** Donald Clarke (ed.) London: Viking, 1989. p. 41

Arroyo, Joe

169. Bradshaw, Paul. "Hey Joe". **Straight No Chaser.** No. 5 (Fall 1989) p. 10

170. McLane, Daisann. "A New Caribbean Generation Sets Listeners to Swaying". **The New York Times** (May 6, 1990) p. 25-H

171. Morales, Ed. "Bumrushed by Joe". **The Village Voice.** Vol. 35, no. 16 (April 17, 1990) p. 87

Azpiazú, Don

172. Roberts, John Storm. "Azpiazú, Don". **The New Grove Dictionary of American Music.** H. Wiley Hitchcock and Stanley Sadie (eds.) London: Macmillan Press, 1986. Vol. 1, p. 100-101

Barretto, Ray

173. "Barretto, Ray". **The New Grove Dictionary of Jazz.**
Barry Kernfeld (ed.) London: Macmillan Press, 1988.
Vol. 1, p. 75-76

174. "Barretto, Ray". **The Penguin Encyclopedia of
Popular Music.** Donald Clarke (ed.) London: Viking, 1989.
p. 73-74

175. Jeske, Lee. "Blindfold Test: Ray Barretto". **Down Beat**
(December 1979) p. 63

176. Margetts, Michelle M. "Ray Barretto: Sometimes the
Path Can Be a Treadmill". **Drums and Drumming.** Vol. 3,
no. 3 (Summer 1987) p. 10-11

177. Roberts, John Storm. "Barretto, Ray". **The New Grove
Dictionary of American Music.** H. Wiley Hitchcock and
Stanley Sadie (eds.) London: Macmillan Press, 1986. Vol.
1, p. 153-154

Record Reviews
Can You Feel It (Atlantic)
178. **Down Beat** (December 21, 1978) p. 36
Cuna, La
179. **Stereo Review.** Vol. 47 (May 1982) p. 50
Ricanstruction (Fania)
180. **Nuestro.** Vol. 4 (May 1980) p. 50
Tomorrow: Barreto Live
181. **Down Beat** (April 21, 1977) p. 30

Bataan, Joe

182. "Bataan, Joe". **The Penguin Encyclopedia of Popular
Music.** Donald Clarke (ed.) London: Viking, 1989. p. 81

Batacumbele

183. Watrous, Peter. "Soundings: Jazz That Speaks Latin, and Vice Versa". **The New York Times.** Vol. 139 (March 18, 1990) sec. 2, p. H31(N)

Bauzá, Mario

184. "Bauzá, Mario". **The New Grove Dictionary of Jazz.** Barry Kernfeld (ed.) London: Macmillan Press, 1988. Vol. 1, p. 83

185. "Bauzá, Mario". **The Penguin Encyclopedia of Popular Music.** Donald Clarke (ed.) London: Viking, 1989. p. 81-82

186. Jackson, David. "Mario Bauzá". **Caribe.** Vol. 6, no. 3, p. 13-15

187. Mieres, Jorge. "Mario Bauzá, Creador del Afrocuban Jazz". **Canales.** Vol. 17, no. 321 (January 15, 1989) p. 26-28

Betancourt, Justo

188. "Betancourt, Justo". **The Penguin Encyclopedia of Popular Music.** Donald Clarke (ed.) London: Viking, 1989. p. 104-105

Blades, Rubén

189. "Blades, Rubén". **Current Biography Yearbook.** 1986. p. 49-53

190. "Blades, Rubén". **The Penguin Encyclopedia of Popular Music.** Donald Clarke (ed.) London: Viking, 1989. p. 115

191. Bloom, Pamela. "A Rubén Blades Close-Up". **High Fidelity.** 36 (April 1986) p. 75

192. Bloom, Pamela. "Discovering Rubén Blades". **High Fidelity** (August 1984) p. 74

193. Cocks, Jay. "The Keen Edge of Rubén Blades". **Time** (July 2, 1984) p. 82

194. Cocks, Jay. "Of Ghosts and Magic". **Time** (July 10, 1988) p. 52

195. DePalma, Anthony. "Rubén Blades: Up from Salsa". **New York Times Magazine** (June 21, 1987) p. 24, 26, 28, 30, 32

196. Fernández, Enrique. "Chilling Out with Rubén Blades". **The Village Voice** (March 5, 1985) p. 79

197. Fricke, David. "Rubén Blades's Latin Revolution". **Rolling Stone** (April 23, 1987) p. 36-39, 158

198. García, Guy D. "Salsa: Rubén Blades". **Interview** (April 1986) p. 210

199. García, Guy D. "Singer, Actor, Político". **Time.** Vol. 135, no. 5 (January 29, 1990) p. 70-72

200. Gehr, Richard. "Partner in Crime". **Music and Sound Output** (May 1988) p. 20-26, 78

201. Ichaso, León (Director). **Crossover Dreams.** Miramax Films, 1985.

Music Score written, arranged and conducted by Mauricio Smith. Additional arrangements by Javier Vázquez, Andy & Jerry González. Musical Consultant: Tony Sabournin. With Virgilio Martí, Andy González, Yomo Toro, Johnny Colón y su Orquesta, Manny Oquendo y Libre, Javier Vázquez, Ray Romero e Izzy Sanabria.

Blades, Rubén (cont.)

202. Levin, Eric. "A Novelist's Eye, a Humanist's Heart and a Hot Band Make Rubén Blades Salsa's 'Número Uno'". **People Weekly** (August 13, 1984) p. 75-76

203. Mieres, Jorge. "'I Will Never Be a Super Star', Says Rubén Blades". **Canales.** Vol. 18, no. 334 (February 15, 1990) p. 54-55

204. Mugge, Robert. **The Return of Rubén Blades.** Sony, 1988. Video, color, 82 min.

Reviews:
205. **The Nation.** Vol. 249 (July 17, 1989) p. 102
206. **The New York Times** (February 21, 1989) p. H30
207. **People Weekly.** Vol. 30 (July 4, 1988)

208. Obejas, Achy. "Rubén Blades: Crosses Over with Nothing but the Truth". **Hispanic** (July 1988) p. 18-23

209. Parker, Robert A. "The Vision of Rubén Blades". **Américas** (March/April 1985) p. 15

210. Sabournin, Tony. "Blades, Rubén". **The New Grove Dictionary of American Music.** H. Wiley Hitchcock and Stanley Sadie (eds.) London: Macmillan Press, 1986. Vol. 1, p. 227

Record Reviews
Agua de Luna (Elektra)
211. **Audio** (November 1987) p. 164
212. **New York Times, The** (January 28, 1987) p. C24(L)
213. **People Weekly** (March 30, 1987) p. 26-27
214. **Rolling Stone** (March 26, 1987) p. 134
215. **Village Voice, The** (February 24, 1987) p. 72
Antecedente (Elektra)
216. **Rolling Stone** (December 15, 1988) p. 200 (2)
217. **Straight No Chaser.** No. 6 (Winter 1989) p. 26-27, 29
218. **Village Voice, The** (January 3, 1989) p. 75

Buscando América (Elektra)
219. **Down Beat.** Vol. 51 (November 1984) p. 31 (2)
220. **People Weekly** (May 7, 1984) p. 26 (2)
221. **Popular Music.** Vol. 6, no. 2 (May 1987) p. 252-255
222. **Rolling Stone** (June 7, 1984) p. 50-51
223. **Stereo Review** (October 1984) p. 98
224. **Time** (July 2, 1984) p. 82
Crossover Dreams (Soundtrack) (Elektra)
See 221
Escenas (Elektra)
See 221
Maestra Vida (Fania)
See 221
Mucho Mejor (Fania)
See 221
Nothing but the Truth (Elektra)
225. **People Weekly** (April 4, 1988) p. 22
226. **Rolling Stone.** No. 526 (May 19, 1988) p. 166
227. **Stereo Review** (October 1988) p. 101
228. **Wilson Library Bulletin.** Vol. 63 (December 1988)
    p. 102
Que la Hace la Paga, El (Fania)
See 221

Bobo, Willie

229. "Bobo, Willie". **The New Grove Dictionary of Jazz.**
Barry Kernfeld (ed.) London: Macmillan Press, 1988.
Vol. 1, p. 131-132

230. "Bobo, Willie". **The Penguin Encyclopedia of Popular Music.** Donald Clarke (ed.) London: Viking, 1989.
p. 130

231. Feather, Leonard. "Blindfold Test: Willie Bobo". **Down
Beat** (December 25, 1969) p. 38

232. Feather, Leonard. "Blindfold Test: Willie Bobo". **Down
Beat** (August 11, 1977) p. 35

Boloña, Sexteto

233. Santos, John. Liner notes to **La Historia del Son Cubano - The Roots of Salsa, Vol. 1. Sexteto Boloña.** Folklyric Records 9053

Record Reviews
Historia del Son Cubano: The Roots of Salsa. Vol. 1 Sexteto Boloña, La (Folklyric)
234. **Sound Choice.** No. 10 (Winter 1989) p. 59, 61

Byrne, David

235. Hanahuer, Mark. "Speaking in Tongues". **Rolling Stone.** No. 569 (January 11, 1990) p. 48, 66

Talks about Byrne's latest foray into Latin music.

Record Reviews
Rei Momo (Luaka Bop/Sire)
236. **Down Beat.** Vol. 57, no. 1 (January 1990) p. 11-12
237. **Rolling Stone.** No. 566 (November 30, 1989) p. 111, 113
238. **Straight No Chaser.** No. 6 (Winter 1989) p. 26-27, 29

Cachao (Israel López)

239. Cota, Juan Carlos. "Cachao". **Down Beat.** Vol. 50 (January 1991) p. 14

240. "López, Israel 'Cachao'". **The Penguin Encyclopedia of Popular Music.** Donald Clarke (ed.) London: Viking, 1989. p. 722

241. Pace, Robert and Lizette Amado. "Cachao - The Original Mambo Man". **Ear.** Vol. 13, no. 4 (June 1988) p. 22-23

Record Reviews
Cachao y su Descarga
242. **Down Beat** (May 18, 1978) p. 30

Camero, Cándido

See   **Cándido**

Camilo, Michel

243. Doerschuk, Bob. "Off the Record: Michel Camilo".
Keyboard (September 1989) p. 59-61

Transcription of the unaccompanied introduction to
"Caribe" from **Michel Camilo** (Portrait/CBS)

244. Grogan, David. "Introducing...: Michel Camilo, who
Returned to his Latin-flavored Jazz Roots when He Left
Santo Domingo". **People Weekly.** Vol. 31, no. 22 (June 5,
1989) p. 91-92

245. Pareles, Jon. "5 Latin Pianists Taking Salsa's Beat
Uptown". **The New York Times** (April 4, 1986). p. 15(N),
p. C1, 9 (L)

Reunion of Eddie and Charlie Palmieri, Hilton Ruiz,
Michel Camilo and Papo Lucca.

246. Potter, Jeff. "Profile: Michel Camilo". **Down Beat.**
Vol. 53 (June 1986) p. 47-48

247. "Santa [Sic] Domingo Swing". **Straight No Chaser.**
No. 5 (Fall 1989) p. 48-49

Record Reviews
Michel Camilo (Portrait/CBS)
248. **Modern Drummer** (July 1989) p. 98
249. **Rhythm** (March 1989) p. 48

Camilo, Michel (cont.)

> **Record Reviews (cont.)**
> On Fire (Epic)
> 250. **Modern Drummer** (April 1990) p. 90
> 251. **Rhythm** (February 1990) p. 46-47
> Suntan (Pro Jazz)
> 252. **Modern Drummer** (August 1987) p. 105

Cándido

> 253. "Camero, Cándido". **The New Grove Dictionary of Jazz.** Barry Kernfeld (ed.) London: Macmillan Press, 1988. Vol. 1, p. 183
>
> 254. "Cándido". **Jazz: The Essential Companion.** Ian Carr, Digby Fairweather and Brian Prestley (eds.) London: Grafton Books, 1987. p. 75
>
> 255. "Cándido". **The Penguin Encyclopedia of Popular Music.** Donald Clarke (ed.) London: Viking, 1989. p. 199
>
> 256. Sanabria, Bobby. "Cándido: Legendary Conguero". **Highlights in Percussion.** Vol. 3, no. 1 (Winter 1988) p. 1-2

Cardona, Milton

> 257. Torres, J. L. "Playing for the Gods: Interview with Milton Cardona and José Mangual Jr.". **Latin New York Magazine** (November 1976)
>
> 258. Wentz, Brooke. "Cuban Rites Drummer Milton Cardona". **Option.** No. K2 (Nov/Dec 1986) p. 37-39

Changuito (José L. Quintana)

259. "Changuito: Un Embajador de la Percusión Cubana". **Sonoc** (Havana, Cuba) No. 2 (1987) p. 12-13

260. Silverman, Chuck. "Inspiration from Manny Oquendo and Changuito". **Highlights in Percussion.** Vol. 5 (Spring/-Summer 1990) p. 12-14

See   Van Van, Los

Cohen, Martin

261. Mattingly, Rick and Adam Budofsky. "Latin Percussion's Martin Cohen". **Modern Drummer.** Vol. 13, no. 9 (September 1989) p. 32-35, 96-97

> Even tough Mr. Cohen is not himself a musician his role in the development of Latin music worldwide is an essential one.

Colón, Willie

262. Agudelo, Carlos. "Salsa para el Nuevo Mundo". **Más.** Vol. 3, no. 5 (September/October 1991) p. 82

263. "Colón, Willie". **The Penguin Encyclopedia of Popular Music.** Donald Clarke (ed.) London: Viking, 1989. p. 266

264. Córdova-Ferrer, Jacqueline. "A Conversation with Willie Colón". **Nuestro** (April 1985) p. 36

265. Fernández, Enrique. "Colonization". **The Village Voice.** Vol. 34, no. 5 (January 31, 1989) p. 78

266. Mieres, Jorge. "Willie Colón: 'Héctor Lavoe Contribuyó a mi Imagen de Malo'. **Canales.** Vol. 17, no. 322 (February 15, 1989) p. 126-128

Colón, Willie (cont.)

267. Roberts, John Storm. "Colón, Willie". **The New Grove Dictionary of American Music.** H. Wiley Hitchcock and Stanley Sadie (eds.) London: Macmillan Press, 1986. Vol. 1, p. 474-475

Record Reviews
Tiempo Pa'Matar (Fania)
268. **People Weekly** (August 20, 1984) p. 20
Top Secrets/Altos Secretos (Fania)
269. **Ear Magazine.** Vol. 14, no. 6 (September 1989) p. 54

Cortijo, Rafael

270. "Cortijo, Rafael". **The Penguin Encyclopedia of Popular Music.** Donald Clarke (ed.) London: Viking, 1989. p. 283-284

271. Rodríguez Juliá, Edgardo. **El Entierro de Cortijo.** Río Piedras, Puerto Rico: Ediciones Huracán, 1983. 96 pp.

Excellent chronicle of the services of Rafael Cortijo. Even though it is intended as a literary work it contains a lot of useful data about Cortijo and his Combo and gives an good insight of the social and musical event that is the death of a famous musician in Puerto Rico.

Cruz, Celia

272. Cooper, Carol. "Our Lady of Perpetual Salsa". **Voice Rock and Roll Quarterly.** Vol. 3, no. 3 (Fall 1990) p. 23-27

273. "Cruz, Celia". **Current Biography Yearbook** (1983) p. 71-74

274. "Cruz, Celia". **The Penguin Encyclopedia of Popular Music.** Donald Clarke (ed.) London: Viking, 1989.
p. 304-305

275. Flores, Aurora. "Celia Cruz: Salsera Sonera". **¿Cómo Yo me Llamo?: Celia Cruz / A Biographical Exhibition of the Life and Artistry of Celia Cruz.** New York, NY: Caribbean Cultural Center, 1990

276. Sabournin, Tony. "Cruz, Celia". **The New Grove Dictionary of American Music.** H. Wiley Hitchcock and Stanley Sadie (eds.) London: Macmillan Press, 1986.
Vol. 1 , p. 553

277. Valverde, Umberto. **Reina Rumba: Celia Cruz.** Mexico: Editorial Universo, 1982. 150 pp.

> Biography of Celia Cruz through interviews with her and collaborators like Johnny Pacheco and the musicians from Sonora Matancera.

Cuba, Joe

278. "Cuba, Joe". **The Penguin Encyclopedia of Popular Music.** Donald Clarke (ed.) London: Viking, 1989.
p. 305-306

Record Reviews
Joe Cuba Sextette
279. **High Fidelity.** Vol. 38 (November 1988) p. 89

Cugat, Xavier

280. "Cugat, Xavier". **The Penguin Encyclopedia of Popular Music.** Donald Clarke (ed.) London: Viking, 1989.
p. 306-307

281. Roberts, John Storm. "Cugat, Xavier". **The New Grove Dictionary of American Music.** H. Wiley Hitchcock and Stanley Sadie (eds.) London: Macmillan Press, 1986.
Vol. 1, p. 553-554

D'León, Oscar

282. "D'León, Oscar". **The Penguin Encyclopedia of Popular Music.** Donald Clarke (ed.) London: Viking, 1989. p. 346-347

D'Rivera, Paquito

283. Cocks, Jay. "Hot Bop from a Tropical Gent: Sax Player Paquito D'Rivera Soars High on an Expatriate Dream". **Time.** Vol. 123 (February 6, 1984) p. 68

284. "D'Rivera, Paquito". **The New Grove Dictionary of Jazz.** Barry Kernfeld (ed.) London: Macmillan Press, 1988. Vol. 1, p. 307

285. Feather, Leonard. "Blindfold Test: Paquito D'Rivera". **Down Beat** (December 1982) p. 55

Record Reviews
Blowin' (Columbia)
286. **Down Beat** (March 1982) p. 34, 36
Explosion (Columbia)
287. **Down Beat** (May 1986) p. 36
Live at the Keystone Corner (Columbia)
288. **Down Beat** (January 1984) p. 32
Manhattan Burn (CBS)
289. **Digital Audio** (April 1988) p. 73
Mariel
290. **Down Beat.** Vol. 50 (April 1983) p. 32
291. **Stereo Review** (January 1983) p. 81
Why Not! (Columbia)
292. **Modern Drummer** (March 1985) p. 67

See   **84. Paquito D'Rivera Music Minus Me**

Enrique, Luis

293. Aguilar, Wilson. "Luis Enrique: 'La Salsa Ha Cambia-do'". **Canales.** Vol. 16, no. 318 (October 10, 1988) p. 10-11

294. Del Barco, Mandalit. "El Salsero Moderno." **Más.** Vol. 1, no. 3 (Spring 1990) p. 68-69

295. Lenart, Nina. "Luis Enrique". **Mambo Express Magazine.** Vol. 3, no. 21 (July 1990) p. 21-22

Faílde, Miguel

296. Castillo Faílde, Osvaldo. **Miguel Faílde, Creador Musical del Danzón.** Havana: Consejo Nacional de Cultura, 1964

Fajardo, José

297. "Fajardo, José Antonio". **The Penguin Encyclopedia of Popular Music.** Donald Clarke (ed.) London: Viking, 1989. p. 403

Fania All Stars

298. "Fania All Stars: Salsa '78 - Crossover or Die". **Down Beat.** Vol. 45, no. 18 (November 2, 1978) p. 17

299. "Fania All Stars". **The Penguin Encyclopedia of Popular Music.** Donald Clarke (ed.) London: Viking, 1989. p. 405-406

300. **Fania All Stars Songbook.** Hialeah, FL: Columbia Pictures Publications, 1978. 112 pp.

> Includes "The Story of the Fania All Stars" by Jerry Massuci (p. 14-15), the official story. Bilingual.

Fania All Stars (cont.)

Record Reviews
Delicate and Jumpy
301. **Down Beat** (December 16, 1976) p. 31
Social Change
302. **Down Beat** (April 1983) p. 32

Fe, Alfredo de la

303. Shinner, Jo. "Techno Salsero". **Straight No Chaser.**
No. 8 (Summer 1990) p. 48-50

Record Reviews
Alfredo (Criollo)
304. **Down Beat** (January 1981) p. 45

Feliciano, Cheo

305. "Feliciano, Cheo". **The Penguin Encyclopedia of
Popular Music.** Donald Clarke (ed.) London: Viking, 1989.
p. 411-412

Fischer, Clare

306. "Fischer, Clare". **The New Grove Dictionary of Jazz.**
Barry Kernfeld (ed.) London: Macmillan Press, 1988. Vol.
1, p. 387

Record Reviews
Salsa Picante (Discovery)
307. **Down Beat** (August 1981) p. 43-44

Formell, Juan

See   **Van Van, Los**

Gillespie, Dizzy

308. "Gillespie, Dizzy". **The Penguin Encyclopedia of Popular Music.** Donald Clarke (ed.) London: Viking, 1989. p. 463-464

309. König, Wolfgang. "The Diz Cuba Connection". **Straight No Chaser.** No. 5 (Fall 1989) p. 40-41

Description of the birth of "Manteca" by Chano Pozo and Dizzy Gillespie that can be seen in 1. Dratch, Howard and Eugene Rosow (Directors). **Routes of Rhythm with Harry Belafonte.**

310. Owens, Thomas. "Gillespie, Dizzy". **The New Grove Dictionary of American Music.** H. Wiley Hitchcock and Stanley Sadie (eds.) London: Macmillan Press, 1986. Vol. 2, p. 220-222

González, Andy

311. Birnbaum, Larry. "Salsa Bassist of the Stars". **Guitar Player.** Vol. 24 (April 1990) p. 10-11

González, Jerry

312. Birnbaum, Larry. "Profile: Jerry González". **Down Beat** (April 1984) p. 56-58

Record Reviews
Obatalá (Enja)
313. **Down Beat** (May 1990) p. 39-40
River is Deep, The (Enja)
314. **Down Beat** (July 1983) p. 40-42
Ya Yo Me Curé (American Clavé)
315. **Down Beat** (February 1982) p. 34, 39

See   183. Watrous, Peter. "Soundings: Jazz That Speaks Latin, and Vice Versa"

Gran Combo, El

316. Alemán, Miranda. "Rafael Ithier y su Gran Combo". **La Klave** (Puerto Rico) Vol. 1, no. 2 (Summer 1989) pp. 18

317. Cotto, Cándida. "¡Acángana!: Entrevista a Rafael Ithier, Director Musical de El Gran Combo". **En Rojo (Suplement of Claridad)** (Puerto Rico) (July 31, 1987) p. 18, 23

318. "El Gran Combo". **The Penguin Encyclopedia of Popular Music.** Donald Clarke (ed.) London: Viking, 1989. p. 378-379

Guerra, Juan Luis

319. McLane, Daisann. "Juan Luis Guerra + 4.40". **Más.** Vol. 3, no. 3 (May/June 1991) p. 72-75

See   170. McLane, Daisann. "A New Caribbean Generation Sets Listeners to Swaying"

Habanero, Sexteto

Record Reviews
Historia del Son Cubano: The Roots of Salsa. Vol. 2. Sexteto Habanero, La (Folklyric)
320. **Sound Choice.** No. 10 (Winter 1989) p. 61
321. **Musician** (January 1988) p. 96

Hanrahan, Kip

322. Bradshaw, Paul. "Anger, Passion and Sexuality". **Straight No Chaser.** No. 8 (Summer 1990) p. 42-43

323. Kalbacher, Gene. "Kip Hanrahan". **Down Beat.** Vol. 51, no. 3 (March 1984) p. 47-48

324. Wentz, Brooke. "Kip Hanrahan's Multilingual Music".
Option. No. K2 (November/December 1986) p. 36-39

Record Reviews
Conjure: Music for the Texts of Ishmael Reed
325. **Down Beat** (December 1983) p. 59
Coup de Tete (American Clavé)
326. **Down Beat** (September 1982) p. 32-33
327. **Musician** (March 1982) p. 80
Days and Nights of Blue Luck Inverted (Pangaea)
328. **Option** No. 22 (September/October 1988) p. 101-102
Desire Develops an Edge (American Clavé)
329. **Down Beat** (March 1984) p. 28-29
Vertical's Currency (American Clavé)
330. **Down Beat** (October 1985) p. 31-32

Harlow, Larry

331. Birnbaum, Larry. "Larry Harlow". **Down Beat** (April 1982) p. 53-54

332. "Harlow, Larry". **The Penguin Encyclopedia of Popular Music.** Donald Clarke (ed.) London: Viking, 1989. p. 514-515

Irakere

333. "Irakere". **The New Grove Dictionary of Jazz.** Barry Kernfeld (ed.) London: Macmillan Press, 1988. Vol. 1, p. 565-566

Record Reviews
Chekere Son (Milestone)
334. **Down Beat** (September 1982) p. 27-28
335. **Stereo Review.** Vol. 47 (August 1982) p. 84
Coco, El
336. **Stereo Review.** Vol. 48 (June 1983) p. 96
337. **Down Beat.** Vol. 50 (April 1983) p. 29

Irakere (cont.)

> **Record Reviews**
> Irakere (Columbia)
> 338. **Down Beat** (May 3, 1979) p. 22

See   Sandoval, Arturo
          Valdés, Chucho

Jorrín, Enrique

> 339. Martínez, Marlén. "Señor Cha Cha Chá: Una Entrevis-
> ta con el Creador de ese Ritmo sin Igual". **Sonoc** (Havana,
> Cuba) No. 3 (1987) p. 6-7

Lavoe, Héctor

> 340. "Lavoe, Héctor". **The Penguin Encyclopedia of
> Popular Music.** Donald Clarke (ed.) London: Viking, 1989.
> p. 687-688

> 341. Sabournin, Tony. "Riffs: Hector Lavoe, Salsa's
> Phoenix". **The Village Voice.** Vol. 25 (September 10, 1980)
> p. 64

> 342. Sullivan, Dita. "El Supermán de la Salsa". **Más.**
> Vol. 1, no. 2 (Winter 1989) p. 66

See   266. Mieres, Jorge. "Willie Colón: 'Héctor Lavoe Contribuyó a mi Imagen
          de Malo'

Legarreta, Félix "Pupi"

> 343. "Legarreta, Félix 'Pupi'". **The Penguin Encyclopedia
> of Popular Music.** Donald Clarke (ed.) London: Viking,
> 1989. p. 694-695

Libre, Conjunto

344. "Libre (Conjunto Libre)". **The Penguin Encyclopedia of Popular Music.** Donald Clarke (ed.) London: Viking, 1989. p. 705-706

Record Reviews
Tiene Calidad
345. **Steppin' Out.** No. 4 (March 13, 1978) p. 3

See   Oquendo, Manny

López, Israel

See   Cachao

Lucca, Papo

346. Alava, Silvio. "Bebop Spoken Here". **Latin Beat.** Vol. 1, no. 2 (February 1991) p. 14-15

Discusses Papo Lucca's involvement with Latin jazz.

347. Birnbaum, Larry. "Caught: Eddie Palmieri/ Hilton Ruiz/ Papo Lucca". **Down Beat** (August 1987) p. 52-53

348. Doerschuk, Robert L. "'Como Mango': A Salsa Piano Solo by Papo Lucca". **Keyboard.** Vol. 15, no. 7 (July 1989) p. 70-71

Transcription, part of Doerschuk, Robert L. "Secrets of Salsa Rhythm: Piano with a Hot Sauce". *See 597*

349. "Lucca, Papo". **The Penguin Encyclopedia of Popular Music.** Donald Clarke (ed.) London: Viking, 1989. p. 726-727

See   Sonora Ponceña
245. Pareles, Jon. "5 Latin Pianists Taking Salsa's Beat Uptown"

Machito

350. Birnbaum, Larry. "Machito: Original Macho Man". **Down Beat** (December 1980) p. 25-27

351. "Machito". **Current Biography Yearbook.** 1983

352. "Machito". **Jazz: The Essential Companion.** Ian Carr, Digby Fairweather and Brian Prestley (eds.) London: Grafton Books, 1987. p. 311

353. "Machito". **The New Grove Dictionary of Jazz.** Barry Kernfeld (ed.) London: Macmillan Press, 1988. Vol. 2, p. 64

354. "Machito". **The Penguin Encyclopedia of Popular Music.** Donald Clarke (ed.) London: Viking, 1989. p. 743-744

355. Ortiz, Carlos (Director). **Machito: A Latin Jazz Legacy.** Nubia Music Society, 1987. Film, 54 min.

Excellent testimonies of Machito and other greats about the origins of Latin jazz.

Reviews:
356. **New York Times, The** (August 28, 1986) p. 17(N)
357. **Wire.** No. 49 (March 1988) p. 13

358. Roberts, John Storm. "Machito". **The New Grove Dictionary of American Music.** H. Wiley Hitchock and Stanley Sadie (eds.) London: Macmillan Press, 1986. Vol. 3, p. 148-149

359. Smith, Arnold Jay. "Sounds from the Salsa Source: Tito and Machito". **Down Beat.** Vol. 43, no. 8 (April 22, 1976) p. 16, 42

Record Reviews
Machito and His Salsa Big Band 1982
360. **Down Beat.** Vol. 50 (April 1983) p. 32

Machito Meets Terry
361. **Down Beat** (May 6, 1976) p. 9

Mangual, José Sr.

Record Reviews
Buyú (Turnstyle)
362. **Down Beat** (December 1, 1977) p. 30

Mangual, José Jr.

See   257. Torres, J. L. "Playing for the Gods: Interview with Milton Cardona and José Mangual Jr"

Mantilla, Ray

363. "Mantilla, Ray". **The New Grove Dictionary of Jazz.** Barry Kernfeld (ed.) London: Macmillan Press, 1988. Vol. 2, p. 81

364. Smith, Arnold Jay. "Ray Mantilla". **Down Beat** (December 15, 1977) p. 44, 46

Record Reviews
Mantilla (Inner City)
365. **Down Beat** (December 21, 1978) p. 36

Martínez, Sabú

366. "Martínez, Sabú". **The New Grove Dictionary of Jazz.** Barry Kernfeld (ed.) London: Macmillan Press, 1988. Vol. 2, p. 88

Mercado, Ralph

367. Rivera, Frankie. "El Poder detrás de la Tarima". **La Klave** (Puerto Rico) Vol. 1, no. 2 (Summer 1989) p. 10

Moré, Benny

> 368. Naser, Amin E.. **Benny Moré.** Havana: Ed. Unión, 1985
>
> Biography of the great cuban singer. It has some useful if spare information about his musical style.
>
> 369. "Moré, Benny". **The Penguin Encyclopedia of Popular Music.** Donald Clarke (ed.) London: Viking, 1989. p. 824
>
> 370. Ruiz Quevedo, Rosendo. "Benny Moré". **Latin Beat.** Vol. 1, no. 3 (March 1991) p. 16-19

Niche, Grupo

> 371. "Grupo Niche". **The Penguin Encyclopedia of Popular Music.** Donald Clarke (ed.) London: Viking, 1989. p. 494-495

Nieves, Tito

> 372. Veira, Juan Ignacio. "Penas y Alegrías de Tito Nieves". **Canales.** Vol. 19, no. 351 (July 1991) p. 6-8

O'Farrill, Chico

> 373. "O'Farrill, Chico (Arturo)". **Jazz: The Essential Companion.** Ian Carr, Digby Fairweather and Brian Prestley (eds.) London: Grafton Books, 1987. p. 372
>
> 374. "O'Farrill, Chico". **The New Grove Dictionary of Jazz.** Barry Kernfeld (ed.) London: Macmillan Press, 1988. Vol. 2, p. 265
>
> 375. "O'Farrill, Chico". **The Penguin Encyclopedia of Popular Music.** Donald Clarke (ed.) London: Viking, 1989. p. 870

Olivencia, Tommy

376. "Olivencia, Tommy". **The Penguin Encyclopedia of Popular Music.** Donald Clarke (ed.) London: Viking, 1989. p. 872-873

Oquendo, Manny

See   **Libre, Conjunto**
260. Silverman, Chuck. "Inspiration from Manny Oquendo and Changuito".

Ortiz, Luis "Perico"

377. "Ortiz, Luis 'Perico'". **The Penguin Encyclopedia of Popular Music.** Donald Clarke (ed.) London: Viking, 1989. p. 878-879

Record Reviews
Super Salsa (New Generation)
378. **Down Beat** (October 1979) p. 38, 42
My Own Image (Turnstyle)
See 378

Pacheco, Johnny

379. "Pacheco, Johnny". **The Penguin Encyclopedia of Popular Music.** Donald Clarke (ed.) London: Viking, 1989. p. 886-887

380. Roberts, John Storm. "Pacheco, Johnny". **The New Grove Dictionary of American Music.** H. Wiley Hitchock and Stanley Sadie (eds.) London: Macmillan Press, 1986. Vol. 3, p. 458

Palmieri, Charlie

381. "Palmieri, Charlie". **The Penguin Encyclopedia of Popular Music.** Donald Clarke (ed.) London: Viking, 1989. p. 889-890

382. Rodríguez, Nancy. "Tribute to Charlie Palmieri". **Latin Beat.** Vol. 1, no. 3 (March 1991) p. 22-24

Record Reviews
A Giant Step (Tropical Budda)
383. **High Fidelity** (May 1985) p. 82-83

Palmieri, Eddie

384. Fernández, Enrique. "Music: Gang of Five". **The Village Voice.** No. 31 (April 15, 1986) p. 79

385. McDonough, Jack. "Eddie Palmieri: King of Salsa Piano". **Contemporary Keyboard** (December 1977) p. 18, 48

386. Newton, Edmund. "Eddie Palmieri, Salsa Man". **The New York Post** (September 27, 1975) p. 13

387. "Palmieri, Eddie". **The Penguin Encyclopedia of Popular Music.** Donald Clarke (ed.) London: Viking, 1989. p. 890-891

388. Primack, Bret. "Blindfold Test: Eddie Palmieri". **Down Beat** (April 19, 1979) p. 31

389. Roberts, John Storm. "Eddie Palmieri on Salsa". **Stereo Review** (February 1976)

390. Roberts, John Storm. "Palmieri, Eddie". **The New Grove Dictionary of American Music.** H. Wiley Hitchcock and Stanley Sadie (eds.) London: Macmillan Press, 1986. Vol. 3, p. 465-466

391. Roberts, John Storm. "Salsa's Prodigal Sun: Eddie Palmieri". **Down Beat** (April 22, 1976) p. 21-22, 42-43

392. Rockwell, John. "Latin Music, Folk Music and the Artist as Craftsman: Eddie Palmieri". **All American Music: Composition in the Late Twentieth Century.** New York: Alfred A. Knopf, 1983. p. 198-208

393. Thompson, Robert Farris. "New Voice from the Barrios". **Saturday Review.** (October 28, 1967) p. 53

Record Reviews
Eddie Palmieri (Bárbaro)
394. **Down Beat** (April 1982) p. 38-40
Lucumí, Macumba, Voodoo (Epic)
395. **Down Beat** (January 11, 1979) p. 24
Palo Pa'Rumba (Musica Latina)
396. **High Fidelity** (May 1985) p. 82-83
Sueño (Intuition/Capitol)
397. **Down Beat** (March 1980) p. 33
398. **Guitar Player** (October 1989) p. 148
399. **Option** (November/December 1989) p. 93
400. **People Weekly** (May 29, 1989) p. 22

See   347. Birnbaum, Larry. "Caught: Eddie Palmieri/ Hilton Ruiz/ Papo Lucca"
245. Pareles, Jon. "5 Latin Pianists Taking Salsa's Beat Uptown".

Papines, Los

401. "Papines Come to States, Los". **Down Beat** (October 20, 1977) p. 10

402. "Papines: Manos de Seda, Poetas del Cuero, Los". **Sonoc** (Havana, Cuba) No. 4 (1987) p. 18

Patato (Carlos Valdés)

403. "Valdés, Carlos 'Patato'". **The New Grove Dictionary of Jazz.** Barry Kernfeld (ed.) London: Macmillan Press, 1988.

Patato (Carlos Valdés) (cont.)

Record Reviews
Ready for Freddy
404. **Down Beat** (June 2, 1977) p. 28

Peraza, Armando

405. "Peraza, Armando". **The New Grove Dictionary of Jazz.** Barry Kernfeld (ed.) London: Macmillan Press, 1988. Vol. 2, p. 301-302

406. Tolleson, Robin. "Santana's Percussion: A Profile in Latin Artistry". **Modern Drummer** (October 1982) p. 12-15, 74-77, 79

Pérez Prado, Dámaso

407. "Prado, Pérez". **The Penguin Encyclopedia of Popular Music.** Donald Clarke (ed.) London: Viking, 1989. p. 929-930

408. García Ascot, Jomí. "Pérez Prado". **Con la música por dentro.** México: Martín Casillas, 1982. p. 156-158

> Interesting analysis of Pérez Prado's contributions and experiments with Afro-Cuban rhythmic structures and big band jazz harmonies.

409. Roberts, John Storm. "Prado, Pérez". **The New Grove Dictionary of American Music.** H. Wiley Hitchcock and Stanley Sadie (eds.) London: Macmillan Press, 1986. Vol. 3, no. 619

Ponce, Daniel

410. "Ponce, Daniel". **The Penguin Encyclopedia of Popular Music.** Donald Clarke (ed.) London: Viking, 1989. p. 925-926

411. Gourse, Leslie. "Ignacio Berroa and Daniel Ponce". **Modern Drummer** (January 1984) p. 57, 61-63

Record Reviews
Arawe (Antilles)
412. **High Fidelity** (May 1988) p. 70-71
New York Now (Celluloid)
413. **Down Beat** (January 1984) p. 32

Ponceña, Sonora

414. Sullivan, Dita. "Riffs: Sonora Ponceña, all of the Above". **The Village Voice** (September 20, 1983) p. 70

See   Lucca, Papo

Pozo, Chano

415. "Pozo, Chano". **The New Grove Dictionary of Jazz.** Barry Kernfeld (ed.) London: Macmillan Press, 1988. Vol. 2, p. 330

416. "Pozo, Chano". **The Penguin Encyclopedia of Popular Music.** Donald Clarke (ed.) London: Viking, 1989. p. 929

417. Roberts, John Storm. "Pozo, Chano". **The New Grove Dictionary of American Music.** H. Wiley Hitchcock and Stanley Sadie (eds.) London: Macmillan Press, 1986. Vol. 3, p. 619

418. Salazar, Max. "Chano Pozo, King of Congas". **Nuestro** (April 1980) p. 56

Prado, Pérez

See   Pérez Prado, Dámaso

Puente, Tito

419. Agudelo, Carlos. "Tito Sigue Siendo el Rey". **Más.** Vol. 2, no. 1 (Fall 1990) p. 76

420. Birnbaum, Larry. "Tito Puente: Timbales' Titan". **Down Beat** (January 1984) p. 27-29, 61

421. Gordon, Diane. "Tito Puente: Polyrhythm Pioneer". **Modern Drummer** (April 1990) p. 24-27, 70-73

Includes a transcription by Bobby Sanabria of Puente's solo on "Mambo Beat"

422. Nash, J. "Tito Puente". **Jazz Times** (October 1988) p. 33

423. "Puente, Tito". **Current Biography Yearbook** (1977)

424. "Puente, Tito". **The Penguin Encyclopedia of Popular Music.** Donald Clarke (ed.) London: Viking, 1989. p. 946-947

425. Roberts, John Storm. "Puente, Tito". **The New Grove Dictionary of American Music.** H. Wiley Hitchcock and Stanley Sadie (eds.) London: Macmillan Press, 1986. Vol. 3, p. 656

426. Sanabria, Bobby. "Tito Puente: Long Live the King". **Highlights in Percussion.** Vol. 5 (Spring/Summer 1990) p. 1, 3-6, 22-24

427. Vega, José de la. "Tito Puente". **Temas.** No. 437 (August 30, 1987) p. 30-37

Record Reviews
Goza Mi Timbal (Concord Picante)
428. **Down Beat** (May 1990) p. 39-40
Salsa Meets Jazz: Tito Puente and His Latin Ensemble
429. **Audio.** Vol. 73 (June 1989) p. 150

Sensación
430. **Jazz Journal International** (February 1987) p. 33
Un Poco Loco
431. **Cadence Magazine** (February 1988) p. 81
432. **Crescendo International** (January 1988) p. 30
433. **Jazz Journal International** (February 1988) p. 32

See   359. Smith, Arnold Jay. "Sounds from the Salsa Source: Tito and Machito"

Quintana, José Luis

See   **Changuito**

Ramírez, Louie

434. Mieres, Jorge. "Louie Ramírez: Creador de la Salsa Romántica". **Canales.** No. 342 (October 15, 1990) p. 6-8

435. Ramírez, Jessie and Frankie Rivera. "Louie Ramírez: 'Ese Genio de la Salsa'". **La Klave** (Puerto Rico) (September 1990) p. 6

436. "Ramírez, Louie". **The Penguin Encyclopedia of Popular Music.** Donald Clarke (ed.) London: Viking, 1989. p. 957-958

Revé, Orquesta

437. Lashmar, Paul. "Revé". **Straight No Chaser.** No. 5 (Fall 1989) p. 6

Record Reviews
Explosión del Momento!, La
438. **Option** (March/April 1990) p. 111

Rivera, Ismael

439. Cepero, Juan. "Ismael Rivera 'Plantao' en la Revolución del Negro Puertorriqueño". **El Mundo** (Puerto Rico) (March 18, 1984) p. B5-B6

Rivera, Ismael (cont.)

440. Figueroa Hernández, Rafael. "Ismael Rivera: Análisis Estilístico de la Producción Musical del Sonero Mayor de Puerto Rico". **En Rojo (Supplement of Claridad)** (Puerto Rico) (June 12, 1987) p. 18, 23

Musical analysis of style features of Ismael Rivera with musical notation.

441. Flores, Aurora. "El Sonero Mayor: Ismael Rivera". **Steppin' Out.** No. 10 (November 1978) p. 1, 4, 7

Profile and review of **Esto sí es lo mío** one of his last albums.

442. Nuñez, Armindo. "Los Sones de Ismael Rivera". **En Rojo (Supplement of Claridad)** (Puerto Rico) (June 26, 1976) p. 3-5

443. "Rivera, Ismael". **The Penguin Encyclopedia of Popular Music.** Donald Clarke (ed.) London: Viking, 1989. p. 988-989

444. Rodríguez Martinó, Graciela. "A Golpes de Bata Maelo se nos Va". **En Rojo (Supplement of Claridad)** (Puerto Rico) (May 21, 1987) p. 22-23

Excellent chronicle of the public services of Ismael Rivera

Rivera, Mario

445. Fernández, Enrique. "Mario Rivera Refugee Camp". **The Village Voice** (June 16, 1987)

446. Tamargo, Luis. "Mario Rivera: Struggling Against Traditional Obscurantism". **Latin Beat.** Vol. 1, no. 11 (December 1991/January 1992) p. 11-12

Rodríguez, Arsenio

447. "Rodríguez, Arsenio". **The Penguin Encyclopedia of Popular Music.** Donald Clarke (ed.) London: Viking, 1989. p. 1002-1003

Rodríguez, Tito

448. "Rodríguez, Tito". **The Penguin Encyclopedia of Popular Music.** Donald Clarke (ed.) London: Viking, 1989. p. 1003

Roena, Roberto

449. "Roena, Roberto". **The Penguin Encyclopedia of Popular Music.** Donald Clarke (ed.) London: Viking, 1989. p. 1004

Rosario, Willie

450. Muñiz, Ramón. "La Verdadera Historia de Willie Rosario". **La Klave** (Puerto Rico) (September 1990) p. 28

451. "Rosario, Willie". **The Penguin Encyclopedia of Popular Music.** Donald Clarke (ed.) London: Viking, 1989. p. 1014

Ruiz, Hilton

452. Birnbaum, Larry. "Hilton Ruiz". **Down Beat.** Vol. 54 (September 1987) p. 15

453. Bradshaw, Paul. "On the Road". **Straight No Chaser.** No. 3 (Spring 1989) p. 26-27

Ruiz, Hilton (cont.)

454. Gam, Michael. "Hilton Ruiz: Musical Feedback of Culture and Climate. **Jazziz.** Vol. 6, no. 5 (August/September 1989) p. 22

455. Primack, Bret. "Hilton Ruiz. Bebop & Latin Piano on the Streets of N.Y." **Keyboard** (May 1982) p. 14, 16-17, 19

456. "Ruiz, Hilton". **The New Grove Dictionary of Jazz.** Barry Kernfeld (ed.) London: Macmillan Press, 1988. Vol. 2, p. 401

457. "Ruiz, Hilton". **The Penguin Encyclopedia of Popular Music.** Donald Clarke (ed.) London: Viking, 1989. p. 1021-1022

Record Reviews
Camino (The Road), El
458. **Down Beat** (June 1988) p. 28
459. **High Fidelity** (June 1988) p. 79
Doin' it Right
460. **People Weekly** (August 27, 1990) p. 18
Something Grand (RCA)
461. **Musician** (August 1987) p. 108
462. **Stereo Review** (December 1987) p. 181
463. **Keyboard** (December 1987) p. 16
Strut (RCA/Novus)
464. **People Weekly** (June 12, 1989) p. 30

See   347. Birnbaum, Larry. "Caught: Eddie Palmieri/ Hilton Ruiz/ Papo Lucca"
        245. Pareles, Jon. "5 Latin Pianists Taking Salsa's Beat Uptown"

Sanabria, Izzy

465. Boggs, Vernon W. "Izzy Sanabria: Popularizing Music". **Latin Beat.** Vol. 1, no. 10 (November 1991) p. 14-17

One of the most important non-musicians responsible of the Salsa boom of the 70's.

Sánchez, Poncho

466. Handler, Michael. "Poncho Sánchez". **Down Beat.** Vol. 56, no. 11 (November 1989) p. 14

Profile and review of **La Familia**

467. Rizo, José. "Chatting with Poncho Sánchez, Jazz Conguero". **Highlights in Percussion.** Vol. 5 (Spring / Summer 1990) p. 8-9

Record Reviews
Fuerte
468. **Cadence** (June 1988) p. 81
Poncho (Discovery)
469. **Down Beat** (December 1979) p. 54-55
Sonando (Concord Jazz Picante)
470. **Down Beat** (July 1983) p. 40-42

Sandoval, Arturo

471. Margetts, Michelle M. "Arturo Sandoval". **Windplayer.** Vol. 7, no. 3. p. 10-13, 25, 31

Profile and interview that includes a transcription of 'Ciento Años de Juventud' from Irakere's album **Irakere 2**

472. "Sandoval, Arturo". **The New Grove Dictionary of Jazz.** Barry Kernfeld (ed.) London: Macmillan Press, 1988. Vol. 2, p. 414

Santamaría, Mongo

473. Feather, Leonard. "Blindfold Test: Mongo Santamaría". **Down Beat** (June 21, 1979) p. 45

474. Goldberg, Norbert. "An Interview with Mongo Santamaría". **Percussive Notes** (July 1984) p. 55-58

Santamaría, Mongo (cont.)

475. Roberts, John Storm. "Santamaría, Mongo". **The New Grove Dictionary of American Music.** H. Wiley Hitchcock and Stanley Sadie (eds.) London: Macmillan Press, 1986. Vol. 4, no. 143

476. "Santamaría, Mongo". **The New Grove Dictionary of Jazz.** Barry Kernfeld (ed.) London: Macmillan Press, 1988. Vol. 2, p. 414-415

477. "Santamaría, Mongo". **The Penguin Encyclopedia of Popular Music.** Donald Clarke (ed.) London: Viking, 1989. p. 1035

478. Smith, Arnold Jay. "Mongo Santamaría: Cuban King of Congas". **Down Beat.** Vol. 44, No. 8 (April 21, 1977) p. 19-20, 48

479. Tamargo, Luis. "Mongo Santamaría: Refuting a Baseless Mythology". **Latin Beat.** Vol. 1, no. 10 (November 1991) p. 12-13

Records Reviews
Afro-Indio
480. **Down Beat** (April 22, 1976) p. 24
Red Hot (Columbia/Tappan Zee)
481. **Down Beat** (May 3, 1979) p. 22
Skins
482. **Down Beat** (February 10, 1977) p. 27
Soca Me Nice (Concord Picante)
483. **Cadence** (April 1989) p. 81

Santana, Carlos

484. Roberts, John Storm. "Santana, Carlos". **The New Grove Dictionary of American Music.** H. Wiley Hitchcock and Stanley Sadie (eds.) London: Macmillan Press, 1986. Vol. 4, p. 144

485. "Santana, Carlos". **The New Grove Dictionary of Jazz.** Barry Kernfeld (ed.) London: Macmillan Press, 1988. Vol. 2, p. 415

486. "Santana". **The Penguin Encyclopedia of Popular Music.** Donald Clarke (ed.) London: Viking, 1989. p. 1035-1036

Record Reviews
Amigos
487. **Down Beat** (October 7, 1976) p. 22
Festival
488. **Down Beat** (April 21, 1977) p. 23
Swing of Delight, The (Columbia)
489. **Down Beat** (January 1981) p. 30

Santarosa, Gilberto

490. Rodríguez Martinó, Graciela. "Gilbertito Santa Rosa... el Insistente". **En Rojo (Supplement of Claridad)** (Puerto Rico) (September 4, 1987) p. 20-21

491. Veira, Juan Ignacio. "Gilberto Santa Rosa: Caballero de la Salsa". **Canales.** Vol. 19, no. 347 (March 1991) p. 30-31

Santiago, Eddie

492. Campos, Fernando. "El Triunfo Irresistible de un Supersalsero: Eddie Santiago". **Canales.** Vol. 17, no. 331 (November 15, 1989) p. 26-28

Socarrás, Alberto

493. Salazar, Max. "Alberto Socarrás: The Color of Music". **Mambo Express Magazine.** Vol. 3, no. 23 (August 1990) p. 4-8

Socarrás, Alberto (cont.)

494. "Socarrás, Alberto". **The New Grove Dictionary of Jazz.** Barry Kernfeld (ed.) London: Macmillan Press, 1988. Vol. 2, p. 477

Típica '73

495. "Típica '73". **The Penguin Encyclopedia of Popular Music.** Donald Clarke (ed.) London: Viking, 1989. p. 1168

Tjader, Cal

496. Roberts, John Storm. "Tjader, Cal". **The New Grove Dictionary of American Music.** H. Wiley Hitchcock and Stanley Sadie (eds.) London: Macmillan Press, 1986. Vol. 4, p. 397

497. "Tjader, Cal". **The New Grove Dictionary of Jazz.** Barry Kernfeld (ed.) London: Macmillan Press, 1988. Vol. 2, p. 539-540

498. "Tjader, Cal". **The Penguin Encyclopedia of Popular Music.** Donald Clarke (ed.) London: Viking, 1989. p. 1169

Record Reviews
At Grace Cathedral (Fantasy)
499. **Down Beat** (August 11, 1977) p. 31
Gozeme! Pero Ya...
500. **Audio** (February 1981) p. 68
Heat Wave with Carmen McRae (Concord Jazz)
501. **Down Beat** (December 1982) p. 36, 38
502. **People Weekly** (September 27, 1982) p. 24
503. **Stereo Review** (December 1982) p. 108
Last Night When We Were Young
504. **Down Beat** (May 20, 1976) p. 29
Onda Va Bien, La
505. **High Fidelity** (May 1981) p. 75
506. **Stereo Review** (July 1980) p. 110

Toro, Yomo

507. Palmer, Robert. "Yomo Toro Blends Latin and Cuban". **The New York Times** (December 25, 1987) p. C27(L)

508. Szabo, Julia. "The King of Cuatro: Interview with Cuatro Player Yomo Toro". **Interview.** Vol. 20 (August 1990) p. 42

Record Reviews
Funky Jíbaro (Antilles/New Directions)
509. **Option** (September/October 1988) p. 117-118

Torres, Roberto

510. "Torres, Roberto". **The Penguin Encyclopedia of Popular Music.** Donald Clarke (ed.) London: Viking, 1989. p. 1171-1172

Trío Matamoros

511. Rodríguez Domínguez, Ezequiel. **Trío Matamoros: Treinta y Cinco Años de Música Popular Cubana.** Havana: Editorial Arte y Literatura, 1978. 203 pp.

> Historical overview of Trío Matamoros, its music and importance for the Cuban music scene. Includes facsimiles of the original sheet music of their compositions and separated biographies of the three members.

Valdés, Carlos

See   Patato

Valdés, Chucho

512. Brody, Jeanne. "Chucho, le Piano d'Irakere". **Jazz Magazine** (Paris, France) No. 334 (December 1984) p. 90

Valdés, Chucho (cont.)

513. "Valdés, Chucho". **The New Grove Dictionary of Jazz.** Barry Kernfeld (ed.) London: Macmillan Press, 1988. Vol. 2, p. 569

See   Irakere

Valentín, Bobby

514. "Valentín, Bobby". **The Penguin Encyclopedia of Popular Music.** Donald Clarke (ed.) London: Viking, 1989. p. 1192-1193

Valentin, Dave

515. Holden, Stephen. "Sounds around Town: Dave Valentin Quintet". **The New York Times** (July 28, 1989) p. C11

Record Reviews
Legends (GPR)
516. **Down Beat** (April 19, 1979) p. 20
Live at the Blue Note (GRP)
517. **Jazz Forum.** No. 119 (April 1989) p. 54
Two Amigos (GRP)
518. **Windplayer.** Vol. 7, no. 3; p. 27

Van Van, Los

519. "Juan Formell y los Van Van". **Sonoc** (Havana, Cuba) No. 2 (1987) p. 8-9

520. Brody, Jeanne. "Los Van Van". **Jazz Magazine** (Paris, France) No. 372 (June 1988) p. 31

521. Valdés Cantero, Alicia. "Formell en Tres Tiempos". **Latin Beat.** Vol. 1, no. 2 (February 1991) p. 20-23

Record Reviews
Songo (Mango)
522. **Option.** No. 28 (September/October 1989) p. 131

Vargas, Wilfrido

Record Reviews
Música, La (Sonotone)
523. **Music & Sound Output** (Octubre 1987) p. 57-58
Vida, Canción y Suerte (Karen)
See 523

Ventura, Johnny

Record Reviews
Si Vuelvo a Nacer (CBS)
524. **Canales.** No. 312 (April 15, 1988) p. 38

Vilató, Orestes

See   406. Tolleson, Robin. "Santana's Percussion: A Profile in Latin Artistry".

Villalona, Fernandito

525. Campos, Fernando. "El Misterio en torno a Fernandito Villalona". **Canales.** Vol. 19, no. 347 (March 1991) p. 14-15

4

Instruments

Percussion (General)

526. Acuña, Alex. **Drums and Percussion.** Kansas City,
MO: Music Source International (Video, color, 60 min.)

> Valuable approach to advanced techniques for soloing
> on drums, conga and timbales plus some tips on
> independence as applied to latin rhythms. This is
> definitely not the place to get information on basic
> techniques.

527. Amira, John. "South of the Border: Congas and
Caribbean Percussion". **Modern Drummer.** No. 6 (August/-
September 1982) p. 94-95

> Interesting graphic way of explaining the techniques
> and the rhythms.

528. Brown, Thomas A. **Afro-Latin Rhythm Dictionary.**
Van Nuys, CA: Alfred Publishing Co. 48 pp.

> Basic and handy guide for all musicians. Not recom-
> mended as a first-time approach to the rhythms.

Percussion (General) (cont.)

529. Cohen, Martin. **Understanding Latin Rhythms.**
Garfield, NJ: Latin Percussion. 16 pp. (Booklet and record
set)

530. Cohen, Martin. **Understanding Latin Rhythms: Down
to Basics.** Garfield, NJ: Latin Percussion. 16 pp. (Booklet
and record set)

> For many years these were the standard of Latin
> percussion learning materials and they are still very
> useful. The first volume is a great example of the
> interplay of the various rhythmic components but
> assumes a basic understanding of the rhythmic struc-
> tures that are covered on the second volume. The
> booklets include descriptions of the instruments
> (conga, bongo, timbale, guiro, tambora and cowbell)
> and the rhythms (cha-cha-chá, mambo, guaguancó,
> bolero, merengue, bomba, plena, son montuno) with
> musical notation.

531. Díaz, Pedrito. **Percusión Afro-Latina (Tomo I).**
Barcelona, Spain: Antoni Bosch, 1983. 112 pp.

> General introduction to the universe of Afro-Cuban
> rhythms and instruments. Valuable not only because
> it provides the guidelines for the correct execution of
> the rhythms that could be found elsewhere but be-
> cause it provides drills that help the player to get
> accustomed to the rhythmic structure of each sequence
> and promote hand independence. The chapter devoted
> to hand cowbell is excellent.

532. Mater, Hans. **An Introduction to Latin Percussion.**
Essex, England: International Music Publications, 1986. 32
pp.

> Basic but useful.

533. Morales, Humberto and Henry Adler. **How to Play Latin American Rhythm Instruments.** Miami, FL: Belwin, 1966. 132 pp. (Includes a supplementary section by Ubaldo Nieto)

> A classic. Dated but still full of correct information. A very good section on old-style timbale playing. Bilingual text.

534. Pollart, G.J. "Basic Latin Percussion". **Woodwind, Brass & Percussion.** Vol. 24, no. 2 (February 1985) p. 3

> Brief description of the latin rhythm section with some guidance on construction and acquisition.

535. Smith, Ethel. **Latin-American Rhythms for the Percussion Instruments.** London: Ethel Smith Music Co., 1951. 28 pp.

536. Soto, Rolando. **Complementary Percussion.** Venice, CA: TropiCal Productions. (Video, Color)

537. Sulsbrück, Birger. **Latin-American Percussion: Rhythms and Rhythm Instruments from Cuba and Brazil.** Copenhagen: Den Rytmiske Aftenskoles Forlag/Edition Wilhelm Hansen, 1986. 184 pp (Book and three cassettes)

> Excellent introduction to Cuban rhythms and percussion instruments. Three cassettes with the examples of the text are included. Some of these are covered in more detail in Sulsbrück, Birger. **Latin-American Percussion: Rhythms and Rhythm Instruments from Cuba.** *See 538.*

538. Sulsbrück, Birger. **Latin-American Percussion: Rhythms and Rhythm Instruments from Cuba.** Copenhagen, Denmark: Edition Wilhelm Hansen, 1988. (Video (VHS/Beta), color, 45 min.; Booklet with musical notation included; Distributed by DCI Music Video Inc.)

Percussion (General) (cont.)

A complement of Sulsbrück, Birger. **Latin-American Percussion: Rhythms and Rhythm Instruments from Cuba and Brazil** *(See 537)*, it offers a more in-depth view of the Cuban side of the book, with excellent demonstrations by Mr. Sulsbrück. The booklet offers some useful notations of piano and bass ostinatos. Excellent.

539. Tobias, D.A. "Latin American Percussion". **The Instrumentalist** (November 1965) p. 74

Arranging

540. Deutsch, Maury. **How to Arrange for Latin-American Instruments.** New York: New Sounds in Modern Music, 1956. 24 pp.

Dated but useful with sections on notation for the rhythm instruments and clave. Interesting classification of rhythms in slow, moderate and fast.

541. Diamante, Carlos. **Arranging Latin-American Music Authentically: A Reference and Guide to Typical Latin-American Dance Forms with Examples of the Forms Scored for Orchestra.** New York: King Brand Publications, 1948. 39 pp.

Samples of orchestrated rhythms (4 bars normally) with some tips on how to orchestrate.

Bass

542. Goines, Lincoln and Robby Ameen. **Funkifying the Clave: Afro-Cuban Grooves for Bass and Drums.** New York, NY: Manhattan Music, 1990. 63 pp. (Book and cassette set)

For bass this is the best possible book available that deals with salsa-related rhythmic structures. Lincoln Goines goes from basic and traditional bass lines to more complex and contemporary ones incorporating features from almost everywhere in the contemporary scene.

For drums this book takes of where Malabe's **Afro-Cuban Rhythms for Drumset** ends *(See 576)*. Robby Ameen has a very solid knowledge of latin structures that allows him to go further and experiment with different combinations and fusions that work perfectly within a clave-based context. The cassette contains besides all the examples on the text six original charts played with a full band and then minus bass and minus drums. Excellent.

543. Laszlo, Bert and Mark Snyder. **Latin Bass: Contemporary Bass Lines and Music for the Modern Bass Player.** Bryn Mawr, PA: Theodore Presser Co., 1982. 32 pp.

Companion book to **Latin Drumming** by Bert Laszlo *(See 575)*. In some senses more useful than its companion book, but still very limited. It provides some good lines and approaches to mambo and cha-cha-chá but without explanation of how they were done. Interesting approach to bass lines classified in traditional and contemporary. It includes two soundpages.

544. López, Rubén. "La Evolución del Bajo en la Salsa". **La Klave** (Puerto Rico) Vol. 1, no. 1 (September/October 1988) p. 30

Brief overview of the role of the bass in salsa and its development.

545. Manuel, Peter. "The Anticipated Bass in Cuban Popular Music". **Revista de Música Latino Americana/Latin American Music Review.** Vol. 6, no. 2 (Fall/Winter 1985) p. 249-261

Bass (cont.)

Ethnomusicological approach to the study of the role of the bass in Cuban music. Interesting analysis of European and Afro-Cuban sources.

546. Rivera, Inocencio. **Bajo Latino. Bass Player's Guide for Modern Latin Rhythms.** Boston, MA: Reno Music Pub., 1969. 24 pp.

Useful guide to *tumbaos*. Unfortunately the bilingual notes are insufficient and do not even touch basic subjects as the relationship of the clave with the bass line or how to play chord changes.

Batá Drums

547. **Batá y Rumba.** Garfield, NJ: Latin Percussion. (Booklet and record set)

Showcases both the religious and secular roots of Salsa. The notes include a transcription of the record-ed performance.

548. Friedman, Robert Alan. **Making an Abstract World Concrete: Knowledge, Competence and Structural Dimensions of Performance Among Batá Drummers in Santería (Cuba, Puerto Rico, New York).** Ph. D. diss., Indiana University, 1982. 335 pp.

Academic study of Batá drumming in performance events of the African-Cuban religion Santería - inter-esting is the concept of organization of sound as related to religious concepts. Chapter 3 'Performance Roles' describes instrumentation and instrumental roles.

549. Goldberg, Norbert. "Ethnic Percussion: Batá drums". **Percussive Notes.** Vol. 21, no. 2 (January 1983) p. 68-69

Brief introduction to the batá drums and their rhythms.

Bongós

550. Arnez, Chico. **Bongos Made Easy.** New York: New Sounds in Modern Music, 1959. 18 pp.

551. "Bongos". **The New Grove Dictionary of Jazz.** Barry Kernfeld (ed.) London: Macmillan Press, 1988. Vol. 1, p. 135

552. Joe, Montego. "Latin Symposium: Bongos". **Modern Percussionist.** Vol. 1, no. 3 (1985) p. 32-33

553. Joe, Montego. **Plays Conga/Bongos.** USA: Envolve Music Co., 1978. 21 pp.

Basic introduction to the performance of instruments and rhythms of the salsa area. Good illustrations of performing techniques.

554. Kessler, William V. **Bongos and How to Play Them.** New York: Charles Colin, 1969

Clave

555. Ortiz, Fernando. **La Clave Xilofónica de la Música Cubana: Ensayo Etnográfico.** Havana: Editorial Letras Cubanas, 1984. 105 pp.

Thorough analysis of origins, musical role, construction and variations of claves.

556. Sanabria, Roberto 'Bobby'. "Playing the Clave". **Highlights in Percussion.** Vol. 2, no. 2 (Summer 1988) p. 9

Conga (Instrument)

557. Charles, David. **Conga, Bongo and Timbale Techniques Live and in the Studio.** New York: Marimba Productions

558. Cordy, Ernie. "South of the Border: Combining Conga and Drumset". **Modern Drummer** (April 1984) p. 78-79

559. Daraca, Jerry. **Conga Drumming: Disco-Soul-Reggae-Rock.** Ontario, CA: Congeros Publications, 1980. 72 pp. (Book and cassette set)

560. Evans, Bob. **Authentic Conga Rhythms: A Complete Study.** New York: Henry Adler Inc., 1958

561. **How to Play Conga Drums.** Los Angeles, CA: Gon Bops of Calif., Inc.

562. James, Bradley. "Latin Beat". **Rhythm** (June 1988) p. 25-26

563. Joe, Montego. "Latin Symposium: the Conga Drums". **Modern Percussionist.** Vol. 1, no. 2, (1985) p. 24-26

564. Levine, Dave. "A Conga Primer". **Rhythm** (July 1981) p. 78-79

565. Reed, Ted. **Progressive Steps to Bongo and Conga Drum Technique.** Clearwater, FL: Ted Reed

566. Santos, John. "South of the Border: Advanced Conga Drum Workshop". **Modern Drummer.** Vol. 13, no. 9 (September 1989) p. 92

567. Santos, John. "South of the Border: Fundamentals of the Tumbadora". **Modern Drummer** (May 1988) p. 64-65

568. Soto, Rolando. **Advanced Conga.** Venice, CA: TropiCal Productions (Video, color)

569. Soto, Rolando. **Basic Conga.** Venice, CA: TropiCal Productions (Video, color)

570. Weber, Glenn. "Wooden Conga Drums". **Modern Drummer** (January 1989) p. 42-43

> Article on wooden congas manufacturers: Latin Percussion, Gon Bops of California, Valje and Meinl

See   553. Joe, Montego. **Plays Conga/Bongos**

Cowbell (Bell)

571. Mason, David A. "Rock'n'Jazz Clinic: Percussion Colors - Part 1". **Modern Drummer** (April 1984) p. 42-43

> Section on cowbell

572. Wheeler, D. "The Cowbell". **Woodwind, Brass and Percussion.** Vol. 22, no. 5 (1983) p. 12

See   96. Silverman, Chuck. "Latin Beat; More Mambo/Bongo Bell Patterns"

Drumset

573. Fink, Ron. **Latin American Rhythms for the Drumset.** Glenview, IL: Creative Music, 1971

> Definitively dated but good for exercises/variations for the cowbell on the Mambo.

574. Guerrero, Frank 'Chico'. **Latin Sounds from the Drum Set.** Hollywood, CA: Professional Drum Shop

> Even though it is a little bit dated it is still an important source of rhythms applied to the drumset.

575. Laszlo, Bert. **Latin Drumming: Latin-American Rhythms for the Modern Drummer.** Bryn Mawr, PA: Theodore Presser Co., 1982. 32 pp.

Drumset (cont.)

> Companion book to **Latin Bass** by Bert Laszlo *(See 543)* and Mark Snyder. Very limited approach to some rhythms of the salsa sphere (cha-cha-cha, mambo) and others not recognizable but with a feeling close to. Some useful examples for the working drummer even though they are not really authentic. It includes two soundpages.

576. Malabé, Frank and Bob Weiner. **Afro-Cuban Rhythms for Drumset.** New York, NY: Manhattan Music Inc, 1990. 64 pp.

> Excellent method not only for drumset players but to all instrumentalists to understand the basic structures of the rhythms covered: Afro-Cuban 6/8, guaguancó, conga, mozambique, songo and merengue. Of special interest are the chapters on clave, palito, cáscara and cowbell patterns. It includes a glossary, discography and bibliography. The well-produced cassette complements perfectly the text. Highly recommended by any means.

577. Miller, William F. "South of the Border: Salsa for the Drumset". **Modern Drummer** (June 1990) p. 64

578. Santos, John. "South of the Border: Latin Rhythms on Drumset". **Modern Drummer** (November 1987) p. 96-97

579. Silverman, Chuck. **The Drum Set with Afro-Caribbean Rhythms.** San Gabriel, CA: Palito Publishing (3 vols. and cassette)

> A manual for the working drummer full of adaptations of latin rhythms for the drumset. The companion cassette includes play along sections. Very good.

580. Ulano, Sam. **The Thinking Drummer.** New York: Sam Ulano, 1960. 48 pp.

The Latin section covers bolero, bolero-rhumba, cha cha chá, afro-cuban, mambo, merengue, guaracha, conga. Interesting approach to practicing.

581. Weber, Glenn. "South of the Border: Latin Drumset Beats". **Modern Drummer** (February 1987) p. 54

See   526. Acuña, Alex. **Drums and Percussion**
558. Cordy, Ernie. "South of the Border: Combining Conga and Drumset"
542. Goines, Lincoln and Robby Ameen. **Funkifying the Clave: Afro-Cuban Grooves for Bass and Drums.**

Education

582. Bash, L. "Teaching Jazz-Rock and Latin Jazz". **The Instrumentalist** (January 1988) p. 70

583. Comer, John. "Rhythm and Percussion Work in Rock and Latin American Styles". **Pop, Rock and Ethnic Music in School.** Graham Vulliamy and Ed Lee (eds.) Cambridge, MA: Cambridge University Press, 1982. p. 40-55

584. Gaines, Joseph Harry. **Music as Socio-Cultural Behavior: Implications for Cross-Cultural Education -A Case Study.** Ed. D. diss., Columbia University Teachers College, 1989. 181 pp.

Study of the performances of a group of professional musicians in New York as example of cross-cultural education through the use of lecture-demonstrations.

585. Hughes, Stacy Edward. **A Compilation of Afro-American and Puerto Rican Music Materials for Use in the New York City Public Schools.** Ed. D. diss., Columbia University Teachers College, 1987. 187 pp.

Emphasize the role of Afro-American and Puerto Rican music as supportive feature in education.

586. Sulsbrück, Birger, Henrik Beck and Karsten Simonsen. **Salsa Session.** Copenhagen: Den Rytmiske Aftenskoles/-Edition Wilhelm Hansen, 1988. 84 pp.

Education (cont.)

> With the help of a demonstration cassette played by Sulsbrück's own band **Salsa Na Ma** this book provides 12 charts scored for a salsa band (piano, bass, complete latin percussion rhythm section and scores for C, Bb and Eb melodic instruments). Excellent working material for ensembles and arrangers to learn some of the most important rhythms and structures in the salsa tradition . A very well-thought introduction to each of the charts completes the package.

Güira

> 587. Alberti, Luis F. **Método de Tambora y Güira.** Santo Domingo: 1973. 34 pp.

> Thorough method to play merengue. It provides drills to practice various instrumental techniques for the tambora and the güira. The lessons prepare the students for the intricacies of the merengue rhythm with its variations. It also contains scores with melodies and accompaniments to play along with the percussion instruments, besides some licks for the saxophone.

Guitar

> 588. Gore, Joe. "Global Guitar: El Son Cubano". **Guitar Player.** Vol. 23 (August 1989) p. 114

> 589. Gore, Joe. "Global Guitar: Tumbaos Típicos". **Guitar Player** (September 1989) p. 114

> 590. Orozco, Danilo. **La Guitarra Acompañante.** Santiago de Cuba: Editorial Oriente, 1978. 175 pp.

> Geared to the amateur musician it has though very useful step by step descriptions of accompaniments for

traditional Cuban tunes like **Guajira Guantanamera,
¡Cuba, qué linda es Cuba!, Ausencia** and **El que
siembra su maíz** and covers the guajira, bolero and
son.

Improvisation (Soloing)

591. Béhague, Gerard. "Improvisation in Latin American
Musics". **Music Educators Journal.** No. 66 (January 1980)
p. 118-125

> Talks about afro-hispanic traditions of improvisation
> with an in-depth view of rumba and how the quintoist
> invents his/her part

592. **Drum Solos.** Garfield, NJ: Latin Percussion. (3
Records)

> Educational records devoted to drum improvisation.
> Side A features professional latin percussionists
> soloing on top of different rhythms. Side B is exactly
> the same except for the soloists that disappear to leave
> room to play along.

593. Silverman, Chuck. "Latin Beat: Solo motifs". **Rhythm.**
Vol. 1, no. 11 (March 1989) p. 44-45

594. Silverman, Chuck. "Latin Beat: More Solo/Fill Ideas".
Rhythm (December 1989) p. 68-69

Maracas

595. Harrison, Ed. "The Art of Maraca Playing". **Percussive
Notes.** Vol. 28, no. 5 (August 1990) p. 5-7

596. Mason, David A. "Rock'n'Jazz Clinic: Percussion
Colors - Part 2". **Modern Drummer** (May 1984) p. 50-51

> Section on maracas

Piano

597. Doerschuk, Robert L. "Secrets of Salsa Rhythm: Piano with a Hot Sauce". **Keyboard.** Vol. 15, no. 7 (July 1989) p. 66-67, 69-73

Interview with Sonny Bravo and Charlie Otwell on how to play salsa piano. Excellent introduction to clave as related to montunos and the seldom seen subject of harmonic voicings. It includes a selected discography and a transcription of "Como Mango" a piano solo by Papo Lucca. Be sure to read Sonny Bravo's note to the article published on the December 1989 issue, p. 10

598. Gerard, Charles. "Salsa - The Rhythm of Latin Piano". **The Piano Stylist & Jazz Workshop** (August/September 1989) p. 20-21

Saxophone

See   97. Austerlitz, Paul. **A History of the Dominican Merengue, Highlighting the Role of the Saxophone**

Shekere

599. Gerstin, Julian. "The Güiro". **Percussive Notes** (July 1984) p. 54

About the shekere, not güiro as the title says. Construction and playing techniques.

600. Santos, John. "Shékere". **Modern Drummer** (April 1989) p. 72-73

Tambora

See   587. Alberti, Luis F. **Método de Tambora y Güira**

Timbales

601. Reed, Ted. **Latin Rhythms for Drums and Timbales**. Clearwater, FL: Ted Reed, 1960. 27 pp.

> A lot of variations on cowbell and other instruments for different rhythms. Thorough. A working method.

602. Rendón, Víctor. **Timbale Solo Transcriptions**. New York: VR Publication, 1989. 39 pp.

603. Sanabria, Bobby. "A Brief History of the Timbale". **Highlights in Percussion**. Vol. 3, no. 1 (Winter 1988) p. 5-6

604. Santos, John. "South of the Border: Timbal Excursions #1". **Modern Drummer** (February 1989) p. 106

605. "Timbales". **The New Grove Dictionary of Jazz**. Barry Kernfeld (ed.) London: Macmillan Press, 1988. Vol. 2, p. 537

Vibes

606. Mendoza, Víctor. "Vibes in Latin Music". **Percussive Notes**. Vol. 22, no. 5 (July 1984) p. 65-67

Author and Title
Index

Numbers refer to entries not to pages. Titles of recordings are in *italics*.

Subject Index

About the Compiler

RAFAEL FIGUEROA is the founder and director of CONCLAVE, an information progam that maintains a database of Afro-Hispanic music of the Antilles. His book *Pasos sobre el silencio* deals with musical semiotics.

www.ingramcontent.com/pod-product-compliance
Lightning Source LLC
Chambersburg PA
CBHW060348100426
42812CB00003B/1169